THE WARTIME DIARY

Of Edmund Kessler
Lwow, Poland, 1942–1944

D1710991

JEWS OF POLAND

Series Editor: *Antony Polonsky*

ACADEMIC
STUDIES
PRESS

THE WARTIME DIARY

Of Edmund Kessler
Lwow, Poland, 1942–1944

Edited By *Renata Kessler*

Introduction By *Antony Polonsky*

Preface By *David Bossman*
Foreword By *Leon W. Wells*
"Salvation" By *Kazimierz Kalwinski*
"Lusia's Letter" By *Lusia Sicher*
Epilogue By *Renata Kessler*
Afterword By *Sarah Shapiro*

5/6/10

To Linda,
Best Wishes,
Renata Kessler

BOSTON
2010

Library of Congress Cataloging-in-Publication Data

Kessler, Edmund, d. 1985.
    [Przezyc holokaust we Lwowie. English]
    The wartime diary of Edmund Kessler : Lwow, Poland, 1942-1944 / introduction by
Antony Polonsky ; preface by David Bossman ; foreword by Leon W. Wells ; "Salvation"
by Kazimierz Kalwinski ; "Lusia's letter" by Lusia Sicher ; epilogue by Renata Kessler ;
afterword by Sarah Shapiro.
        p. cm. — (Jews of Poland)
    Includes bibliographical references and index.
    ISBN 978-1-934843-98-7 (hbk.) — ISBN 978-1-934843-99-4 (pbk.)
    1. Kessler, Edmund, d. 1985 — Diaries. 2. Jews — Ukraine — L'viv — Diaries. 3.
Jews — Poland — Diaries. 4. Holocaust, Jewish (1939-1945) — Ukraine — L'viv —
Personal narratives. 5. Holocaust, Jewish (1939-1945) — Poland — Personal narratives.
6. Jewish ghettos — Ukraine — L'viv — History — 20th century. 7. Jews — Persecutions
— Ukraine — L'viv — History — 20th century. 8. Janowska (Concentration camp) 9.
Bunkers (Fortification) — Ukraine — L'viv Region — History — 20th century. 10. L'viv
(Ukraine) — Biography. I. Title.
    DS135.U42L855213 2010
    940.53'15092--dc22
    [B]
                                                    2010000597

ISBN 978-1-934843-98-7 (hardback)

ISBN 978-1-934843-99-4 (paperback)

Book design by *Ivan Grave*

Published by Academic Studies Press in 2010

28 Montfern Avenue Brighton,

MA 02135, USA

press@academicstudiespress.com

www.academicstudiespress.com

CONTENTS

CONTINUATION
Poem for Edmund Kessler's Birthday

Your hopes and dreams
Your unfulfilled expectations
Passed on through me
Your continuation.

Your bitter disappointments
The price of life's exactations
Yearn for fulfillment in me
The Second Generation

The words you wrote in secret
About our family
Our people
Our tribulation
Become my revelation

Now we are
One mind
One heart
One purpose

The dignity you were denied
The words that were not said
Find their voice in mine
Where father stops
And daughter starts
I do not know
The hazy lines between life and death
Cannot be explained
I only know the task left unfinished
Still remains

This task defines what I must do
This book, my birthday gift to you
To share the history of our nation
This bond of love
Our continuation.

Written June 2, 2007 by Renata Kessler

Wedding Portrait of Edmund and Fryderyka Kessler
Lwow, Poland, 1937

In memory of my parents, Edmund and Fryderyka Kessler and their rescuers, Wojciech and Katarzyna Kalwinski, who along with their son Kazimierz, risked their lives and those of their family to save twenty-four Jews during the Holocaust.

I would also like to acknowledge my late cousin Henryka Lyszczak, her husband Wiktor Lyszczak, and their friend Jacek Bukowski who encouraged me in this endeavor.

Written in memoriam for Ruth Dorfman and Berta Mandel and all others who perished in the Shoah so that their voices might be heard.

ACKNOWLEDGEMENTS

First and foremost, I would like to acknowledge my father, Edmund Kessler who recognized the historical importance of these events and recorded them in his diary from 1942-1944 in Lwow, Poland. Very important to the book is Kazimierz Kalwinski, son of Wojciech and Katarzyna, who contributed his memories of the bunker and the war years. Two survivors hidden in the Kalwinski bunker, Leon Weliczker Wells and Lusia Sicher, also made written contributions.

My gratitude goes to the late Sister Rose Thering, Father Lawrence Frizzell, and Reverend David Bossman, Ph.D. of the Graduate Department of Jewish-Christian Studies at Seton Hall University, whose guidance and faith in the book proved invaluable.

Special thanks to Dr. Eugene Bergman who translated and edited the original manuscript into English. Additional translation and transcription contributions were made by Przemyslaw Murczkiewicz, who assisted me throughout. His devotion to the book is greatly appreciated. I am also grateful to Michael Skakun, for additional editing of the manuscript. My dearest friend, author, and journalist, Sarah Shapiro (daughter of the late Norman Cousins) made suggestions, offered her expertise along the way, and edited the epilogue. My father's life-long friends Oscar and Lillian Muller deserve recognition for their friendship throughout and their translation of Kazimierz Kalwinski's testimonial tape cassette.

ACKNOWLEDGEMENTS

Thank you Jack Goldfarb for steering me toward the Jewish Historical Institute in Warsaw where I was helped in my endeavor by Historian, Feliks Tych. Edyta Kurek made it possible find my father's true voice with a superb transcription of my father's words which was published by the Institute in the Original Polish language in 2007. I am indebted to Antony Polonsky who recognized the value of the book and wrote the very fine scholarly introduction for the English translation, and to Eva Fogelman for her encouragement.

I would also like to acknowledge Sigmund Rolat of the Museum of the History of Polish Jews. Most supportive were Sara and Rabbi Bald of Lviv, and Meylakh Sheyket, Director of the Union of Councils for Jews of the former Soviet Union in Lviv, who aided me in my research there.

My appreciation to the Kalwinski and Bukowski families for their hospitality during my stay in Poland, and to the Ukrainian family in Lviv who allowed me to visit their home, the former Kalwinski house. My heartfelt thanks to George Tschurjumow, and to all my relatives, colleagues, and friends for their love and support in this endeavor.

PREFACE

Reverend David M. Bossman, Ph.D.

Little more needs to be added to justify ongoing Holocaust studies then the simple question, "Why were six million Jews annihilated during World War II?" Many studies have approached this question with answers ranging from a centuries-old anti-Jewish polemic to an economic crisis that required a scapegoat to deflect responsibility. Most studies do shed light on this highly complex issue in Western history. Some of these even suggest that the Third Reich's "Final Solution" was the most heinous genocide in world history. Are more witnesses needed to drive the point home? Haven't we sufficient information to draw all conclusions necessary for lessons from history? Or is there still a mysterious quality to the Holocaust that remains unexplained? The present book sheds light on this dark mystery in surprising but useful ways.

The Wartime Diary of Edmund Kessler contributes a distinctive perspective to a study of the Holocaust. First, Edmund Kessler was an eye-witness who experienced the war first hand and made notes at the time the events were happening. Second, he was a practicing lawyer whose training enabled him to sort out the details in a meaningful set of observations. Third, this diary finds support today from a gentile who knew Edmund Kessler and assisted him and those others with him during the period of their hiding in Lwow, Poland. Finally, the narrative journal also contains the intense poetry of Edmund Kessler, reflecting on insights and emotions that he drew from his experiences.

Holocaust studies have as their purpose both a recounting of what actually happened as well as developing careful inferences for the future from that history. What actually happened was a panoply of specifics played out over time. No historical moment is created from nothingness but rather is part of a series of ongoing circumstances that frame actions and give them contextual meaning. Some would suggest that the uniqueness of the circumstances tends to disallow meaningful inferences, since meanings inhere in contexts. Yet it is self-evident that historical events take on a life of their own and have an ongoing impact for years to come on the generations which follow. Stereotypes endure beyond the time when it is seen that acting on them can have disastrous consequences. False assumptions can also continue to contaminate people's thinking time after time through a series of historical moments. Scholars need to clarify issues, verify their truthfulness, explore their meanings. The task is as new as each new data emerges for further study. In the case of the murder of the six million, the very vastness of the actions warrant as much data and scholarly effort as resources can afford.[*]

---

[*] **What happened to the Jews of Lwow?** Lwow was the third largest pre-war Jewish community in Poland. Prior to 1939, 110,000 Jews were settled there. During the Nazi occupation of Poland about 100,000 Jews fled to the Soviet occupied zone of Lwow and its environs. Under Soviet occupation some Jews collaborated with the Soviets. Others, were persecuted and deported to Siberia when they refused to take up Soviet citizenship. Jewish political activists were arrested. Following the invasion of the German forces in 1941, the Ukrainians accused Jews of helping the NKVD. The majority of those killed were Polish nationalists, intellectuals, political prisoners, and Ukrainians, as well as Jews. During this four week pogrom nearly 4,000 Jews were killed in Lwow in retribution. Groups of Polish professors from Lvov universities were also killed.

Under the terms of the German — Soviet pact, The Soviet Union occupied the city of Lwow/Lvov from 1939 until the invasion of the Soviet Union by Germany. Subsequently, it was occupied by the Germans who committed some of the most heinous crimes in history against the defenseless Jewish population. When the German army was aware that they were losing the war, they tried to cover up evidence of the mass murders they performed at Janowska and elsewhere's in Europe. It is documented that prisoners were forced to open up mass graves and cremate bodies. Once this was accomplished the remaining prisoners were murdered to obliterate evidence of German crimes.

During the Nazi reign of terror many great round-ups and *Aktions* occurred. Jews were forced into the Ghetto. Selection for hard labor followed by deportations to the death camps was the tragic fate of the Jews of Lwow. By the time the Soviet Army liberated

Now we have this new set of data to advance studies of the Holocaust. The eye-witness account of a skilled observer written on the scene and verified by contemporary witness. We do well to explore these memoirs and to celebrate the energies that went into their preservation and publication. I am pleased to have advised Renata Renee Kessler, daughter of Edmund Kessler, and to have supported her endeavors. She expended great effort in gaining knowledge of her father's home life in Poland, meeting those who knew him, all the while overseeing the translation and transcription of his writings with invaluable assistance from Przemyslaw Murczkiewicz. She also commissioned Dr. Eugene Bergman to translate from the original Polish manuscript to English. The final transcription of the manuscript was done by Edyta Kuric at the Jewish Historical Institute in Warsaw whose expertise helped to reveal the authentic words of Edmund Kessler over the chasm of time. All in all, this process has required total dedication to complete. It is a labor of love but also a significant contribution to the ongoing examination in addressing meaning of the Holocaust for those who were its victims, its survivors, and the heirs of its effects.

Lwow from the Nazis, only 200-300 Jews survived in hiding. Among them was Edmund Kessler, a Lwow attorney, who documented these events contributing his perspective.

It is still difficult to understand how the Germans, respected for their high degree of culture and civilization, were capable of committing such barbarous acts against an innocent civilian population. Edmund Kessler reflects on the backwards evolution of man into an orgy of blood and violence, showing us how thin the human veneer of civilization can be given certain circumstances. Against this background the Kalwinski farmers performed heroic deeds by risking their lives and that of their family to shelter 24 Jews. These circumstances revealed the dual nature of man. — *Renata Kessler.*

FOREWORD

Leon Wells

March 5, 2005

The Wartime Diary of Edmund Kessler was of great interest to me, not only because I was hidden in the same place with Edmund and Fryderyka Kessler, but for many more reasons. The book gave me certain information that I had not previously known. It was written as a diary/memoir and was organized by his daughter, Renata Kessler who was born after the war. She commissioned the translation of the text into English. It also contains a chapter from Kazik (Kazimierz Kalwinski), the son of the people who hid us. Kazik was only fifteen years old when his parents made a hiding place for the Jews and he was aware of the risk to his whole family. For example, when the German troops retreated from Russia and looked in the suburbs of Lwow for a place to stay overnight with their horses, one of the places they investigated was the property where we were hiding. Our "savior" Mrs. Kalwinska with her youngest son Stasiek showed them around. As they passed the clock, the little boy Stasiek, who was about 9 years old pointed it out to his mother, saying loudly, "Look someone is using the electricity!" We in the hiding place had a small bulb which was always on. The mother became frightened, but the German soldiers did not pay attention to this statement. After this incident, the beloved parents decided to send their child away to some relatives in western Poland, bearing in mind that if they were caught at least one member of the family would survive. These relatives did not treat him like a beloved child and it took some time after the liberation of Lwow until he could return. According to the book, the parents explained to him that he was sent away because they wanted to save him. A neighbor was discovered hiding Jews and he was hanged in a city park with a sign on his chest "Hiding Jews."

Edmund Kessler and his wife were part of the Lwow establishment. He had a doctorate of law and she came from a wealthy family. When the Germans took over, the city established a Judenrat, a Jewish committee comprised of well-known leaders. The Kesslers knew more about these Judenrat representatives than my parents or the society from which I came. We were Hasidic Jews who lived in our own community and did not mingle with secular Jews or Christians.

I came to the hiding place much later than the Kesslers did. We slept on the same platform. The entire hideout where we Jews stayed was 9 feet by 15 feet in area. The Kesslers and I slept over the area that was used for a bathroom. To get down one had to hunch as the ceiling was right above us.

Being an eighteen year old boy, I was in awe of this older educated man and his wife. In the hiding place, we all spoke very little except when it was necessary.

Even though much of this part of Poland was Hasidic, this book will be of interest to readers and students of the Holocaust, because it was written by an assimilated Jew. Included is the memoir of the son of a saintly family who saved 24 Jews. They were among the *Righteous Of The Nations*.

Part I

Kessler Family Liquor Business
Lwow, Poland, 1910
Courtesy of Anna Kessler Fiertag.

INTRODUCTION

Antony Polonsky

> I thought deeply, I wondered about the miracle of rescue
> And I found the answer — you are good people.
> Today I know that my survival comes only from the miracle
> That such brave people are found on earth.
>
> Edmund Kessler

On the eve of the Second World War, Lwów (Lviv, Lemberg)* had a Jewish population of over 100,000. The influx of refugees after the Nazi occupation of central Poland increased this number to nearly 180,000. Some Jews managed to flee before the establishment of a ghetto in the city in November 1942. Nevertheless, the Lwów ghetto, which contained at its height at least 105,000 Jews was one of the largest in Europe. Compared to ghettos like those in Warsaw, Łódź or Vilna, it has produced a somewhat limited scholarly literature. Among historical descriptions of the Lwów ghetto, one should mention Philip Friedman, 'The Destruction of the Jews of Lwów', in *Roads to Extinction: Essays on the Holocaust,* ed. Ada June Friedman (New York, 1980), 244-32, Dieter Pohl, *Nationalsozialistische Judenverfolgung in Ostgalizien 1941-1944* (Munich, 1996) and Eliiakhu Iones, *Evrei L'vova v gody vtoroi mirovoi voiny i katastrofy evropeiskogo evreistva 1939-1944,* (ed. Svetlana Shenbrunn, Moscow, 1999). Published memoirs in English are also

---

* Lviv is the city's present name. The city was known as Lwow in Polish, Lvov in Russian and Lemberg in Yiddish and German. The Jewish Community of Lwow dates back to the 13th Century. Lemberg Jewry belonged to the Hapsburg Empire for almost 150 years. The city was long Polish, then became Austro-Hungarian, and was again Polish between World War I and World War II. It was annexed by the Soviets in 1939 after the Soviet-German non-agression pact. From June 30, 1941 until 1944, the city was occupied by Nazi Germany and then taken back by the Soviets and reattached to the Ukraine after the Second World War. — *Renata Kessler..*

not very numerous. They include Leon Weliczker Wells, *The Janowska Road* (New York, 1963), Rabbi David Kahane *Lvov Ghetto Diary*, trans. Jerzy Michalowicz (Amherst, MA, 1990), Jacob Gerstenfeld-Maltiel, *My Private War: One Man's Struggle to Survive the Soviets and the Nazis* (London, 1993) and Joachim Schoenfeld, *Holocaust Memoirs: Jews in the Lwów Ghetto, the Janowski Concentration Camp, and as Deportees in Siberia* (Hoboken NJ, 1985). There is therefore all the more reason to welcome the appearance of this English translation of *Edmund Kessler's diary.** This is made up of three separate documents. The first is Kessler's own account, dating from the period of the occupation, of the persecution, ghettoization, and mass murder of the Jews of Lwów. The second is a series of poems Kessler wrote at this time and the third a memoir, written in 1998 by Kazimierz Kalwiński, the son of Wojciech and Katarzyna Kalwiński, who hid Edmund Kessler, his wife, and twenty-two other Jews in a bunker on his small farm in the suburbs of Lwów where they survived the Nazi occupation. In addition, Renata Kessler provides a moving account of her efforts, sixty years later to investigate her father's story and bring it to a wider audience.

Edmund Kessler was born into a prosperous and acculturated Jewish family in Lwów where he practiced as a lawyer before the war. His native city had a long Jewish history. Jews had lived here since its establishment in the mid-thirteenth century. The first synagogue dated from the late sixteenth century and the largest synagogue from this period — *di goldene roze* — was built in the early seventeenth century. Before the First World War, the town had been the capital of Galicia, an autonomous province of the Austro-Hungarian Empire, a major cultural and educational centre, sophisticated and cosmopolitan, with many echoes of Vienna and Budapest (It was often referred to as 'little Vienna in the East'). In the Polish mind the town became a bastion, *semper fidelis*, which had never surrendered and had always defended Poland-Lithuanians against Tartars, Turks and Cossacks. Here was located Jan Sobieski's residence,

---

* The first publication of Edmund Kessler's diary appeared in the original Polish language as 'Przezyc Holokaust We Lwowie' (To Survive The War in Lwow), Jewish Historical Institute, Warsaw, 2007.

the Bernadine Church, the Lyczakowski cemetery and the graves of those who defended the city against Ukrainians in 1918 and 1919, for which the town was collectively awarded the decoration Virtuti Militari by Piłsudski on 22 November 1920. Here too there was a special type of person, the 'Lwowski batiar' the tough man of the streets, with his characteristic mode of speech.[1]

The bitter conflict over the town and over East Galicia as a whole in the immediate aftermath of the war intensified the patriotism of the local Poles, which often took a perfervid anti-Ukrainian form. According to Kazimiera Saysse-Tobiczek:

> Lwów, that old and steadfast fortress stands firm and steadfast in the conflagration of a war between brothers. Lwów, through the centuries has had one fate, with hardened breast to defend Ruthenian, Polish and Lithuanian land from the invasion of enemy Cossack hordes and a rabble of Wallachians, Turks and Tartars.[2]

Lvovian Jews often felt a strong sense of local patriotism. But this was also frequently undermined by the strength of Polish nationalism here and the large-scale anti-Jewish violence which followed the establishment of Polish rule in the town in November 1918, the revenge taken by Polish troops for the neutral position which the Jews had adopted in the post-war Polish/Ukrainian conflict for control of East Galicia. In his elegiac *Mój Lwów*, published in New York in 1946, the Polish-Jewish writer, Józef Wittlin attempted to describe the essence of his native city — its mixture of the sublime and the street urchin, of wisdom and stupidity, of the elevated and the mundane. He saw this essence as ultimately indefinable, comparing it to a local fruit, the *czereha*, neither cherry nor sour cherry. At the same time he notes ironically, 'Nostalgia likes to falsify taste as well, telling us today to feel only the sweetness of Lwów. But I know people for whom Lwów was a bitter cup.'[3]

In his conclusion, he evokes, only partly ironically, both what united and what divided the city's former inhabitants:

> It is no great feat to love when one belongs to the same clan, nation, or party, when one is united by the same attractions and disgusts.

> Love, friendship, and collegiality begin precisely where stark contrast and oppositions take shape…I cannot… pass by in silence that moment in those fratricidal Polish-Ukrainian battles which cut not only the city into two hostile parts, when my old gymnasium friend, Zenon Rusin, at that time a Ukrainian khorunzhyi (military volunteer), stopped hostilities in front of the Jesuit Garden so that I could cross the front and get home. There was harmony among my friends, even though many of them belonged to various warring nations and held to different beliefs and views. National Democrats got along with Jews, socialists with conservatives, Old Ruthenians and Russophiles with Ukrainian nationalists. There were no communists at that time, but if there had been they would certainly have gotten on well even with the socialists. Let us play at this idyll.[4]

As this quotation makes clear, Lwów was a multi-ethnic city.[5] The figures we have are not wholly accurate, partly because of administrative pressure, particularly after 1918 to downplay the number of Ukrainians and because of the different criteria used in different censuses. In 1910, the population of the town numbered around 206,100. Roman Catholics (for the most part Poles) constituted around 50 per cent, Greek Catholics 19.1 percent and those of the 'Israelite faith' 27.8 percent.[6] The percentage of Greek Catholics had increased from 11.2 per cent in 1857 and the town now became not only a major Polish cultural centre, but also a stronghold of Ukrainian activity, strengthened by the fact that some sixty percent of the population of Galicia east of the San river was Ukrainian, while Poles in this area constituted only 25 per cent.[7]

In the 1880s, the previously dominant pro-German orientation among the Jews of Lwów had been replaced in the 1880s by a pro-Polish one, but this was undermined in the years before 1914 by the growth of anti-Semitism and the Jewish awareness that Ukrainians were a majority in the eastern part of Galicia, which caused growing reluctance to side entirely with the Poles in an increasingly bitter ethnic conflict. On the eve of the First World War, the pro-Polish integrationists in the city were facing a growing challenge from the burgeoning Zionist movement.

Fighting continued around Lwów until the Treaty of Riga in March 1921 and the town suffered considerable damage which was only made good by the mid-1920s.[8] The population soon surpassed its pre-war level reaching 219,300 in 1921 (in a slightly increased area) and 310,300 by 1931.[9] By 1921, the proportion of Ukrainians in the city had fallen 12.4 percent in 1921 while that of Jews had risen to 35 percent. Roman Catholics still comprised about half of the population. By 1931 the proportion of Jews had fallen to 32.1 percent, while the Greek Catholic proportion increased to 15.9 percent. Other ethnic groups were now insignificant. Only half of those who described themselves in 1900 as Germans remained in the city, while the remainder had either emigrated or been assimilated. The assimilation of local Armenians to the Polish majority was also progressing rapidly. In that year 63.5 percent of the town's inhabitants gave their mother tongue as Polish, 7.75 percent gave Ukrainian, 3.5 percent gave Ruthenian, and 24 percent gave Yiddish, and there were small groups of Russian, German, and Czech speakers.[10]

The different ethnic groups lived in close proximity to each other. Ukrainians who earlier mostly in the districts of Halickie Przedmieście (now Halyts'kyi raion) and Lyczaków (Lychakiv) were distributed nearly evenly throughout the city. During the 1920s, Roman Catholics did not make up more than 70 percent of the population in any district of the city. The only area where Jews were a majority was Żólkiewskie Przedmieście but their share of the population here had declined from 64 per cent in 1869, this share declined to 53.5 percent in the 1920s. In no other district did Jews constitute more than half of the population.[11]

The loss of its status as a capital and its geographic location in the extreme south-east of the new country had a negative impact on the economic situation of Lwów. Although it remained the seat of the headquarters of many companies active in Galicia, that representing the oil industry of the region now moved to Warsaw. It proved difficult to establish commercial links beyond the country's frontiers and in in the 1920s the Lwów Fair lost significance in comparison to that in Poznań.

Its cultural life was also adversely affected. The periodical *Biblioteka Lwówska* was only able to publish one issue between 1918 and 1928, while many artists and intellectuals now left the town, most moving to Warsaw.[12]

The local Jews were well-organized. Politically they were divided between the assimilationists who had dominated Jewish life before the First World War and the Zionists who became increasingly strong in the interwar period. On 10 September 1932, a prominent assimilationist Wiktor Chajes observed bitterly that 'assimilation is bankrupt'. A sign of the growing strength of Zionism is the fact that Edmund Kessler, a member of long-established and prosperous family with a home in the historic town square identified with this grouping.

The Jews here, particularly those who were better off, were mostly Polish-speaking. This is reflected in the support they gave to *Chwila*, the local daily Polish-language newspaper intended for Jews which was established in January 1919 by Henryk Rosmarin and David Schreiber, two Sejm deputies from the town in the aftermath of the large-scale anti-Jewish violence which broke out in here in November 1918. By the late twenties its circulation reached 35,000 and in 1934 it established an evening edition. It also published belles-lettres and in the late 1920s a circle of Polish-Jewish writers, including Maurycy Szymel, Stefan Pomer, Anda Eker and Karol Dresdner, was associated with the newspaper. They were given considerable encouragement by the newspaper's literary critic, Izydor Berman.

Although inter-ethnic relations were for the most part peaceful in Lwów, violence did sometimes break out. In the mid-1920s, the Jews here were greatly agitated by the trial of Leon Steiger, who was accused by the Polish authorities of attempting to murder the Polish President Stanisław Wojciechowski during his visit to Lwów in 1924. In fact the assassination attempt had been the work of Ukrainian nationalists, one of whom finally confessed his responsibility in 1925. But the trial had been accompanied by many accusations against the Jews as a whole, which had alarmed the Jewish leadership.[13]

Again in June 1929 only firm action by the Minister of the Interior, Felicjan Sławoj-Skladkowski, prevented the violence provoked by an alleged Jewish profanation of a Corpus Christi procession here from spreading, after an Endek mob destroyed the offices of *Chwila* and the local branch of the Yiddish paper *Der moment* and also attacked the Jewish girls' gymnasium, whose pupils were held to be responsible for the alleged sacrilege and the *Dom Studencki* (Jewish Students' Club).

Lwów was occupied by the Soviets in September 1939 under the terms of the Nazi-Soviet pact. Because of the flight of many refugees to the city, by January 1940 the Jewish population had risen to 180,000. This was reduced by deportations, mainly of refugees, to Siberia and central Asia and on the eve of the German invasion there were approximately 150,000 Jews in the city.

On 30 June, 1941 the German First Mountain Division accompanied by the German *Nachtigall* battalion of Ukrainian nationalist legionnaires entered Lwów. Anti-Jewish violence broke out immediately. The pretext was the discovery of the bodies of several thousand prisoners who had been murdered by the Soviet security forces (NKVD) immediately before they left the town. The Jews were held collectively responsible for these murders and for their alleged collaboration with the Soviets.[14] Einsatzgruppe C and A rapidly organized local Ukrainian militia, made up mostly of people from outside Lwów, and orchestrated a brutal massacre in which at 4,000 Jews were murdered.[15] Kessler's diary gives a horrifying account of these murders. One important detail he brings out is that on this occasion, when asked by Rabbi Kahane to intervene, the Metropolitan of the Greek Catholic Church, Andrei Sheptytsky, refused to speak out against the murders. This was not the end of the murders, which were carried on in early July by German Security Police units and by the auxiliary Ukrainian police force, created out of the militia, which ultimately became a separate Ukrainian police division under Major Volodymyr Pitulej.[16] According to the records of Einsatzgruppe C, between 2,500 and 3,000 Jewish men were shot in the period immediately after the violence in the first days of July.[17]

In late July 1941, further violence was instigated in the 'Petliura Days,' allegedly in response to the fifteenth anniversary of the assassination by a Jewish anarchist of the Ukrainian leader Simon Petliura, in retaliation for his responsibility for the mass killings of Jews by Ukrainian forces during the Russian civil war.[18] Much of the violence was carried out the Ukrainian police force and over 1,000 Jews were killed in very brutal conditions. This event is also movingly described by Kessler. On the day after the pogrom, the German authorities extorted a large 'contribution' from the local Jews which they hoped, as Kessler explains, would stop the recurrence of the violence to which they had been subjected. Throughout the summer additional smaller-scale *Aktions* took place throughout the summer, in which Jews were murdered by the SS in the woods to the east of Łyczakowska Street, in the Lesienice forest to the west or in the so-called Sands (Piaski) near the Janowska Road cemetery.[19]

A Judenrat (Jewish Council) was established in late July 1941.[20] Its members hoped, as it proved vainly, that they would be able to mitigate the harshness of German rule. Dr. Józef Parnas, a lawyer, was the first of four Judenrat chairmen, all of whom were either murdered by the Germans or died of illness. He was succeeded by Drs. Adolf Rotfeld, Henryk Landesberg, and Eduard Ebersohn. The Judenrat's first community publication described twenty-three departments in various locations throughout the city which were responsible for the distribution of rations, housing, and health care and also bore responsibility for filling labor quotas and meeting German demands for 'contributions.' A ban on schooling, public worship, and other cultural activities severely restricted the activities of the educational and cultural divisions, although teaching and worship continued secretly and underground publications appeared.[21]

In September 1941, Hans Frank, Governor General of the *Generalgouvernment*, the Governor of *Distrikt Galizien* Karl Lasch, and Lwów Mayor Hans Kujath began to discuss the setting up of a ghetto in Lwów which led by the end of October to a positive decision. As a result, between 12 November and 15 December, Jews were required to move to the areas assigned to the ghetto, which was set up in the in the Zamarstynów and Kleparów districts, which had large Jewish populations, while Poles and Ukrainians were obliged to leave these areas. Jews were only permitted to take a restricted number of household goods. In all, 80,000 Jews were ordered to move to the ghetto. The difficulties involved in the process led to its suspension in December, leaving some 20,000 Jews still outside the ghetto. The ghettoization process was marked by large-scale looting in which the local population participated, as is graphically described by Kessler. According to Mauricy Allerhand, there was 'unheard of exploitation by the…Ukrainian and, in exceptional cases, also the Polish population.' Non-Jews who obtained an official 'order' for an apartment to be vacated by Jews extorted money for letting them take their moveable property with them. Jews were frequently compelled to vacate their apartments within as little as a quarter or half an hour, causing them to lose most of their moveable property.[22] The forced move was also accompanied by the murder of several thousand Jews, including for the first time women and children.[23]

In order to facilitate the relocation of the Jews, in November 1941, the Germans set up a Jewish police force (*Ordnungsdienst*). One of its four divisions of the Jewish served the Judenrat while the remainder were directly subordinate to the German secret police (Gestapo). By the spring of 1941, it numbered perhaps 750.[24] Initially ghetto opinion was not hostile to the police force, seen as necessary to maintain order in the ghetto, but it soon became hated because of its role in filling labor and deportation quotas and its susceptibility to bribery.[25] At the same time, there does seem to have been at least one attempt within the police to organize a resistance group.[26]

Intercession by the Judenrat established by the Germans and fears of a typhus outbreak meant that the sealing of the ghetto and the move into it of the 20,000 Jews still outside only took place in November 1942.[27] This delay brought no relief to the local Jewish population, because in the intervening period the first large-scale deportation of from Lwów took place when, in March 1942, over 15,000 Jews were taken to the Bełżec death camp. The situation worsened still further in May 1942, when the SS Police Chief for *Distrikt Galizien*, Friedrich Katzmann, assumed responsibility for Jewish affairs and now required Jews on the streets of the town to wear armbands with a Star of David and to possess work certificates.[28]

A second major deportation was organized in August 1942. On this occasion around 42,000 Jews were murdered, some in the city itself, some at Bełżec and some in the SS-run Janowska Road forced labor camp on the northwestern edge of the city.[29] Kessler provides a graphic picture of the appalling conditions which prevailed in this camp. At the end of August, the German authorities estimated that around 50,000 Jews still remained in the city. Katzmann now ordered all those outside the ghetto to relocate by 7 September, proclaiming the 'establishment of a closed Jewish residential district' on 21 August. It was however, only on 10 November that the ghetto was finally sealed. It establishment was accompanied by further brutality. On 1 September, SS-Sturmbannführer Erich Engels publicly hanged the head of the Judenrat, Dr. Landesberg and ten Judenrat officials in reprisal for the killing of a Security Police officer. This marked the effective end of the Judenrat and the reconstituted body was placed in the hands of the Jewish Police.[30]

The ghetto, which was surrounded by a wooden fence, ran from the Pełtew River in the north to Kleparowska Street in the east, Zamarstynowska Street in the west and Rappaporta and Szpitalna Streets in the south. Its gates were guarded by Jewish, Ukrainian, and German police units — the main one stood where Pełtewna Street met the southern edge of the ghetto.[31]

As in other ghettos, Jews came to see working for German firms as the only way to survive the occupation. The found work in numerous private firms run either by local civilians or by Germans which were located outside the ghetto, as well as for the German army and the Ostbahn railway company. These were mostly enterprises contributing to the war effort, such as clothing factories and construction firms. The largest private German firm belonged to a Berlin industrialist, Schwarz, who employed about 3,000 Jews.[32] Shortly before the ghetto was closed, approximately 10,000 Jews were working for the Wehrmacht.[33] The SS ran two forced labor camps: a larger one on Janowska Road and a smaller one on Czwartaków Street. The Organisation Todt ran the comparatively small Persenkowka camp.

As elsewhere in the Generalgouvernement, different parts of the bureaucracy had different attitudes towards the use of Jewish labor. Most hostile was the SS and Police Chief Katzmann. A similar attitude was taken by the German labor office (*Arbeitsamt*).[34] Against this, the Lwów labor office and armaments command (*Rüstungskommando*) was more willing to use Jewish labor to deal with the shortages caused by the deportations of Polish and Ukrainian workers to the Reich.[35]

Resistance in the Lwów ghetto was on a smaller scale than in ghettos such as Warsaw or Vilna until its final liquidation. This was primarily the result of the disruptive effect of the Soviet occupation on Jewish communal solidarity and the demoralizing consequences of the wave of violence which followed the Nazi invasion, creating a gulf between Jews and Ukrainians and, to a lesser extent between Jews and Poles. In addition, the German policy of inflicting collective reprisals inhibited resistance. Some weapons were acquired from Italian and Hungarian soldiers and from sympathetic locals and in late 1942, a group of young Judenrat officials set up underground military training courses. They did not succeed in organizing armed resistance.[36]

Deportations from the ghetto continued during the winter of 1942-1943. In January 1943, according to official German figures, there were still 24,000 Jews in the ghetto, although their real number was probably somewhat higher. After another mass shooting, killing at least 10,000 of the ghetto's inhabitants, the German administration transformed the ghetto into a work camp or (known as *Judenlager*, or *Julag*). The Judenrat was dissolved and its members mostly killed, the remainder being incarcerated in the Janowska Road camp. SS-Hauptsturmführer Josef Grzymek, known for his extreme cruelty, oversaw the *Julag* from mid-February 1943 until its liquidation in June 1943.[37]

By May 1943, the *Julag* (ghetto remnant) contained about 12,000 registered inhabitants. It was liquidated by German and Ukrainian police in June 1943. Some Jews escaped into the sewers, while others fired guns and threw grenades from bunkers. Many committed suicide. Several German policemen were killed. After being driven out of the bunkers by fire, the remaining Jews were taken to the Janowska Road camp, and, after selections, many were shot. Some victims may have been deported to Sobibor. In November 1943, the 3,000 remaining inmates of the Janowska Road camp were killed together with 2,000 Jewish forced laborers of the Ostbahn.[38] The camp itself, now temporarily inhabited by several hundred gentile inmates, continued to exist.

Very few Lwów Jews survived the Nazi occupation. When the town was liberated by the Soviets barely 200-300 Jewish survivors were still to be found. In November 1944, a local Jewish committee estimated that there were 2,500 Jews in Lwów. Not all of these were local and it calculated that of the Jews either born in Lwów or resident there at the time of German occupation, only 823 survived. [39] Most of these, like Edmund and Fryderyka Kessler, did so because of the help of sympathetic and courageous individuals, like the Kalwińskis.[40] Sometimes this assistance was organized. From late 1942, there was a branch in Lwów of Żegota, the Polish Council for Aid to Jews.[41] The head of the Greek-Catholic Church Metropolitan Andrei Sheptytskyi, who spoke out against Ukrainian involvement in the mass murder organized an operation hiding about 150 Jews. Eleven Roman-Catholic monasteries in Lwów are known to have sheltered Jewish children. There were also occasions during Aktions when a Polish or Ukrainian neighbor deliberately told policemen that no Jews remained in the apartment building. Some survivors hid for longer periods in the city, others went to the countryside and hid in peasants' homes. Some individuals also succeeded in escaping deportation by jumping from the trains and escaping into the forest where they were on occasion able to find help.[42] Such people are the few bright lights in the dark picture of human cruelty, hatred and barbarism which emerges from this diary.

THE KESSLER FAMILY OF LWOW

Renata Kessler

The Kessler family goes back for centuries in Lwow, Poland which was formerly called Lemberg and was part of Austria prior to World War I. It is currently known as Lviv, Ukraine and has passed through different national rulers over the centuries, giving it a varied ethnic identity. At the time of my father's birth at the beginning of the twentieth century, there were three major groups in Lwow: Polish, Ukrainian, and Jewish. Each group had its own distinct language and culture. During times of war and political unrest, tensions flared between these ethnic groups.

Little remains of the Jewish population of Lwow after the Holocaust. After the war the surviving Jews, along with Poles, repatriated to Poland. Seeking to escape Communist rule, many Jews migrated to Western Europe, the United States, and Israel.

During the life span of my paternal great-grandparents Moses Elias Kessler and Adela Kurzweiler, Lwow was known as Lemberg in Austrian Galicia. The Kesslers were an assimilated and prosperous family, practicing law, medicine, and business. They lived in historic houses on the town square (*Rynek*) bordering the "Kamienica Czarna," now known as "The Black House" Museum close to the summer palace of the Polish King. One relative was a physician. The Polish King liked having a Jewish doctor. The Kessler family can be traced back several centuries to a relative known as "Adama" or "Adamo" who lived several door away from the King's residence.

According to records from databases provided by the Lviv Archives, Documents of the Jewish Religious Community, P. 701, and lists of the voters to the "Council of the Jewish Religious Community for 1937," and records obtained through the Jewish Historical Institute in Warsaw, my great-grandparents, gave birth to my grandfather, Rachmiel Kessler (Polish name Ryszard) on October 12, 1877, his brother Dawid Kessler, born ten years prior on May 5, 1867, his sister, Zippe, born in 1869 and their brother, Mordche Hersh, born February 24, 1866. Other siblings were Jakob Kessler, born in 1883 (he later became a judge), Zelman Salomon, born in 1887, Charlotte, born in 1887, and Frajda, born in 1879. The Kesslers were a large family destroyed by the Nazi Holocaust.

Several family members converted to Christianity in order avoid oppression and to enjoy opportunities not open to Jews. My father's cousin, Pawel Kessler,* converted with his parents and became a Polish judge. He died in a Soviet prison during a massacre of Polish officials under Russian occupation and was buried in a mass grave in Winnica, 1940 (not far from Katyn). To preserve his memory, his name is inscribed on a tomb of the family grave where my Aunt Maria Jasinska (nee Matylda Kessler) and her daughter, Henryka Lyszczak with her husband Wiktor are buried in the Warsaw Catholic Cemetery. The grave is maintained by their dearest friends the Bukowski family.

My father, Edmund Kessler, was a Jewish attorney. He was born at the beginning of the twentieth century to Rachmiel Kessler (also known by his Polish name as Ryszard Kessler) and his wife Laura (nee Frankel). Edmund's older sister Adela died in the Holocaust along with her husband, and her two sons, Natan and Alexander. His younger sister Maria Kessler Jasinska (also known as Manya and Matylda) survived the war with her daughter Henryka, who later became a prominent economist for the Polish government. Her husband Wiktor was a lawyer for the Polish Parliament. My Aunt Manya converted early in life to marry a Catholic cousin, Stanislaus Kessler Jasinski. Henryka was baptized in the Polish Catholic Church, but spent much of her life

---

* Pawel Kessler is mentioned on the Katyn Memorial Wall.

fearing the discovery of her Jewish roots. It was only on her deathbed that she acknowledged her Jewish heritage and called for a Rabbi.

My Grandfather was said to be a charming man who dressed well. My father loved him dearly, and often told me stories of his childhood experiences. Unfortunately, I was deprived of the experience of knowing him. He died during the murder of Jews in the Lwow Ghetto, followed by the death of his wife Laura.

During his lifetime, Ryszard was a merchant in the family liquor businesses. Prior to WWII, he was Director of the well-known firm *Muszynski, Jan I S-ka zo.o. Fabryka Likierow i Wodek,* producing Polish liquors, vodka, and rum since 1894. Co-directors were Markus Kellner and Natan Stern. In 1922, this information was documented in a business directory, *Ksiega Adresowa Przemyslu Handlu I Finansow.* The address of this company was listed as Lwow, Grodzickich 3.

My grandfather was also the director of the firm, *Polonia*, which was located on the *Rynek* in Lwow and produced liquor, rum, and beer. He was also connected with Lwow's *Baczewski, Fabryka wodek i likieru* whose products were well known all over Poland and Europe prior to the Second World War.

My great uncle Dawid Kessler worked as a merchant on trading ships. He lived in Liverpool during the reign of Queen Victoria and worked as an apprentice in a Polish distillery based in Liverpool where he learned his skills, later putting them to use in the family business when he settled in Lwow. He often told stories about seeing Queen Victoria in London, riding through the crowds on a white horse.

Dawid divorced his first wife who later died in London. He remarried his children's governess, Hanna Kaye who was from a poor but educated Jewish family. Since it was difficult for her parents to arrange a marriage, she became a teacher. She had taught in a children's village in Switzerland. Dawid had hired her to teach his children languages. She married Dawid and became the mother of his son, Juliusz Henryk .

Dawid and Rachmiel Kessler were brothers. Juliusz grew up with my father, Edmund Kessler. They played together as children and kept in contact after the war. Juliusz Henryk, later known as Julian Henry attended a selective Polish school. According to his daughter (my cousin Anna), his classmates were the sons of aristocracy and bright sons of manual workers. As a child he suffered from the anti-Semitic comments of the other children. He had been a military cadet, and joined the army as an officer when he left school. He played with the army football team. He also attended Warsaw University and studied economics and law. He was unsuccessful at law, but his real passion was for painting. He shared a studio with other artists. While in Warsaw, he painted backdrops at the Opera House. He continued to pursue his artistic interests throughout his life and also collected antiques which he proudly showed me during my first visits to London.

When the Germans invaded Poland, he was captured, but escaped and returned to Lwow, only to be arrested again when the Russians invaded. This time he was tried and sentenced to hard labor in Siberia as a political prisoner. He spent two and a half years in Russian labor camps. He spent the time of his prison term building railways, mining precious metals, and in solitary confinement. Needless to say, he suffered from the treatment he received from the Soviets.

When the Russians joined the allies he was released and joined the Polish army. He became the leader of the non-Catholic forces and was made the Chief Rabbi. Juliusz Kessler was the only secular university educated Jew that was wanted for the job. Later, he joined the British armed forces. He returned to Britain and received honors for his military service. He was also awarded a concession in St. James Park in London, near Buckingham Palace which he built into the well-known "Cake House."

In the summer of 2004, I traveled to Lviv, Ukraine (formerly Lwow, Poland) with his daughter to rediscover our family roots. More is written about this journey in my Epilogue which tells about my search for the past. My father's story is revealed in his autobiographical statement and in his wartime journal about the Nazi reign of terror.

AUTOBIOGRAPHICAL STATEMENT

Edmund Kessler

With additions by Renata Kessler

My name is Edmund Kessler. I was born in Lwow Poland. Before the war I lived in Lwow at 12 Sykstuska Street. This was a house built sometime in 1938. I moved there after its completion, having my apartment and my law office there, as well. Until 1938, I lived at 30 Kopernika Street, where likewise my office was.

Sykstuska Street was in the city center. My apartment in that house included two rooms set aside for my office. The house also contained residential and office quarters for two attorneys. I had a telephone line.

In 1939 Lwow was occupied by Russian troops and I had to give up my practice. I also had to give up my apartment and was allocated to another dwelling in the same house. To be allowed to resume my law practice, I had to submit an official application that was to be considered publicly. Since I was known in Lwow as an activist in a Jewish nationalist organization, I would be threatened with exile to Siberia were I to submit that application. Therefore, I dared not submit it.

To make ends meet, I took a job at the Nationalized Gastronomic Organization (Restaurant-Trust). I worked there as a statistician and then as an economist. The organization was associated with 200-300 gastronomic establishments for which it had to prepare an overall plan. I worked in a subordinate capacity for drafting that plan. Thus, I worked at the organization's central office rather than at any particular restaurant.

I believe that it was on the 29th or 30th of June, 1941 that Lwow became occupied by German troops. I did not flee, because I lacked the opportunity for doing so, and also because my family was against it. Naturally, I lost my job. I stayed home so as not to attract attention, and later I found a job with a Jewish charitable organization. Even before the summer of 1941 was over, Germans detained me in the street, took me for forced labor and beat me brutally. Afterward, I again worked in the soup kitchen. During the summer of 1941 we had to leave our home. After staying a day or two with my mother we found a place to stay at my sister's along with my mother, because she had also been evicted. We stayed there for about three or four weeks. During that time, one night all of our possessions were looted from us by the Ukrainian police, the Schutzpolizei or the SS.

Three or four weeks later we all had to leave my sister's home and move to the Zniesienie district of Lwow, which was to be incorporated into the Ghetto. There, the eight of us in the family lived in a single room for several weeks. Afterward, I was able to obtain a room in a house owned by a friend in the Ghetto. My friend was my former schoolmate, Dr. Johann Jankowski. His house was on Tetmajara 15. Together with my wife, my brother-in-law, and my father-in-law, we moved into that room. That happened in October 1941. There were two Lembergs (Lwow). Life outside and inside the Ghetto. In the Ghetto, life was very hard.

Sometime in Spring of 1942, I was again detained and beaten until unconscious, and in that condition was carried home. In the meantime, more "razzias" (raids) to capture Jews took place; one in March 1942 and another in June 1942. I found that working in the soup kitchen did not protect me from deportation and therefore took another job, which I found with a German Red Cross office in the Lwow Railroad Station, as a laborer.

At the end of August or the beginning of September 1942, I was again arrested, and this time taken to the Lwow-Janowska Concentration Camp. In that camp I spent three months. I was often beaten there and had to work very hard. Food was scant. We received coffee, one liter of soup, and 100 grams of bread daily. These were the supposed rations, but in reality we received even less. I was assigned to stone work. We were housed in the camp's barrack.

Later in the Autumn of 1942, I succeeded in escaping from the camp. I proceeded to the dwelling of Polish friends of mine in Lwow. They had already been hiding my wife, Fryderyka since August 1942 when I was still in the concentration camp. My wife was hidden there in an attic with several other people. Among them were Mrs. Sicher and her daughter Lusia.

In June or July of 1943 the Lwow Ghetto was liquidated. The family, who had witnessed the liquidation, could no longer endure the tension and asked us to leave the hideout (they have not given permission to release their names). Their situation was aggravated by the fact that some neighbors became suspicious and began to talk. We then recalled where Mrs. Sicher and her daughter were hiding with a farmer named Kalwinski. After we beseeched him insistently, he permitted us to join them in the hide out, which he had built under a pig-pen. The hideout measured 5 x 7 meters in area and was inhabited by 18 persons. With us four the number rose to 22. In November two more people joined us. In the end there were 24 people. Needless to say, in this situation life was very difficult, but somehow we managed to survive until the liberation on the 27th of July, 1944.

The story of my own and my wife's survival is a long and complicated one. But in general, we owe our survival to two gentile families who risked their lives and that of their families to give us protection during the period of August 1942 until July 27, 1944. It was their expression of compassion for other human beings.

After the liberation, my wife and I returned to our old home on Sykstuska Street. After four days we were about to be evicted by the Red Army. One of the officers billeted with us and we were alowed to remain. My health was in very bad condition. I could barely walk and crawled around on all four legs. After I managed to recover to some degree, I got my old job back at the Restaurant-Trust.

In March 1945, I applied for repatriation to Poland. We took a train to Rzeszow and stayed there with my acquaintances, the Silber family, on

Galezowskiego Street until another pogrom erupted. Together with all other Jews in the city, my wife and I were detained. Sometime in June we moved to Krakow. There we found a place to stay with an acquaintance of mine, Mr. Weiner, whom I accidentally met on the street. Sometime in the fall of that year we found an apartment on Wielopole Street. We had to give it up after a short time, thereupon moving to 2 Filipa Street.

While in Krakow, I tried to resume my law practice, but was not allowed to practice as counsel for defense, because of my reputation as a Jewish nationalist. As a result, I was deprived of my source of income as a lawyer. I survived from a limited civilian law practice and a small amount of two hundred dollars which I received from assets of my parents-in-law, which we sold for a very meager sum out of desperation. However, in Krakow too, a pogrom took place. Under the circumstances, I realized I could not provide a decent living for my family. My wife was almost seven months pregnant when we traveled to Vienna, Austria.

On arriving in Vienna, I landed in the refugee camp on Arzberger Street. After spending a short time at the Camp's Rothschild Hospital, I found an apartment at 2 Lerchengasse. Later we found a more permanent dwelling.

While in Vienna, I worked as secretary and later as Chairman for the International Committee for Jewish Refugees and Concentration Camp Internees, whose office was located on Weringerguertel. The Committee administered the refugee camps in Vienna and processed over 200,000 Jews. I worked for the Committee from 1946 until 1952 and was recognized for my efforts by the American Joint Distribution Committee (see letter, March 15, 1952), the U.S. High Commission, the Austrian Government, and the IRO.

We emigrated to the United States in April of 1952. I have kept various notes and written a history of the Lwow Ghetto, my experiences in the Janowska Concentration Camp, and of the cellar hide-out in the Kalwinski bunker. These experiences were written between 1942-1944, in Lwow, Poland. These records were all written in the Polish language.

LIFE IN AMERICA

Renata Kessler

My family and I arrived in the US when I was only five years old. I remember the huge culture shock and disorientation that my parents experienced when arriving into a new world where they were strangers, barely over their traumatic blows and losses in Europe's Holocaust. I also remember the inspiring image of hope made by the Statue of Liberty, as our ship pulled into New York Harbor.

My father had wanted to fulfill his boyhood dream of settling in the Jewish homeland. However, my mother, devastated by the war in Europe was unable to face the challenges of building a new life in *The Promised Land.*

We were sponsored by a boyhood friend of my father's who had escaped to America prior to the war. He had done well in America and lived in a beautiful apartment in New York overlooking Central Park. There were also relatives from Rzeszow who had arrived here before the 1920's that welcomed us. Of course, they wanted to know more about what happened to the Jews of Europe. This was not considered fit conversation for young children and was talked about behind closed doors. I was later told about the Christian families who saved my parents during the war, when my parents thought I was old enough to understand such things. I was about nine or ten, when my parents lit yitzkor lights for my grandparents on Yom Kippur and told me that my grandparents, aunts, uncles, and cousins were murdered during the war.

My parents told me that they had survived due to the brave deeds of a noble Polish farmer and his family. I was given the abbreviated version. They spared me many of the sordid details about the war which I was to learn almost fifty years later from my father's diary and from the son of their rescuers.

After our arrival in the U.S. we had a short stay in a hotel and several rooming houses in New York. Later we settled in a three room apartment in Manhattan's upper west side. My father worked at American Express as an international travel agent from approximately 1953-1959. He planned itineraries for tourists and businessmen traveling to Europe. My father spoke five languages: Polish, German, Russian, English, and Hebrew. He was familiar with Europe. Being well-spoken and sociable, he was well suited for the job. Even though my father enjoyed this work, it made an inadequate living to support a family.

Therefore, he decided to continue his education. Even though my father had been a lawyer in Poland, he did not consider studying law in the U.S. which was entirely different. I remember asking him why he had not become a lawyer in the U.S. He told me that his foreign accent might prejudice a jury against his client. Also, I suspect that studying a different law in a new country might have proved to be too much after all that he had endured in Europe. Toward the end of his life he mentioned that he had not realized at the time that there were many different kinds of law that could be practiced without going to court. There were regrets. My father felt that he had not lived his full potential in life due to circumstances of the war. He suffered from depression. He had been torn from his native Poland, and had not fulfilled his boyhood dream of building a Jewish homeland. He entered into a strange new culture to which he had to adjust. Thinking it was too late practice law in the U.S., he settled for a career in accounting. He received a Masters of Business Administration from New York University in June, 1958. He worked as an accountant for New York State, and later for the New York City Department of Rent and Rehabilitation. He retired in the 1980's.

When my parents first arrived in America, the atmosphere was not conducive to publishing a book about the Holocaust. During the McCarthy witch-hunts, Edmund was apprehensive about communicating with his sister and niece behind the iron curtain in Poland.

As it thawed their communication was renewed. Also, many people in America did not want to hear about the pain of the European Jewry immediately after the war. It was not until the much later that books about this subject began to appear.

Upon reading *The Janowska Road* (formerly *The Death Brigade)* by Leon Wells, my mother felt that my father should publish his own diary written in the Lwow Ghetto and the bunker where they were hidden. Even though I was a teenager at the time, we transcribed several pages of my father's diary and translated them. I had read *The Diary of Anne Frank* and became aware of the parallels between the Frank family and my own. However, reliving these events proved to be too much for my father. He felt apprehensive about what the results of opening the door to the past would be, so the project lay dormant for years. I myself was ambivalent about my Holocaust past. It was then the 1960's. I wanted to pursue the "American Dream" and leave all those dark thoughts of the past behind me — but I could not. It was always there hovering over me like a dark cloud separating me from the brilliance and immediacy of life. On some level, I wanted to pretend it never really happened until I reached maturity. Maturity came late to me, in part, because of my inability to accept this past. It has taken me almost sixty years to come to terms with the reality of the Holocaust and anti-Semitism; both past and present.

As my father approached the final years of his life, my mother, who recognized the value of the diary, again encouraged him to translate it into English and publish it before it was too late. By this time my father was too old and too ill to deal with the job. I remember my mother's words to my father: "What you did not do, Renata will do, she inherited your gift for writing."

My father died shortly afterwards, but these words remained and planted the seed that has now come to fruition. After my mother's death in 1996 the Diary resurfaced in a maze of papers and letters I found in her apartment.

Thus began the long journey that landed me in the Jewish Historical Institute in Warsaw on April 22, 2008, to celebrate the publication of *Przezyc Holokaust We Lwowie (Surviving The Holokaust in Lwow)*. Filled with anticipation, I addressed the audience of historians and other academics at the Institute. Historian Feliks Tych contributed his expertise to the seminar. As Director of the Jewish Historical Institute, he felt a moral responsibility to publish my father's diary. After reading the text, he told me that he himself was a hidden child. It was his story as well. The circumstances may have been different, but the story was the same.

My father's diary written during his years of hiding in Poland is a rare treasure. It is yet another vehicle that has the potential to bring out more of the hidden children who live in Poland and elsewhere today. It also shows that during great danger ordinary people can do extraordinary things. Could I have been as brave as this family was? This is a difficult question to answer, because we never know who we really are until we are tested.

NOTES

1   On L'viv see, J. Wereszyca (ed.), Semper fidelis — wiersze o Lwowie (Warsaw, 1986; S. S. Niceja, Cmentarz Łyczakowski we Lwowie w latach 1786-1986 (Wrocław, 1988); idem, Cmentarz Obrońców Lwowa (Wrocław, 1990);

2   Quoted in Kolbuszewski, 236.

3   Józef Wittlin, Mój Lwów (New York, 1946), 8. For a very stimulating account of the literary images evoked by Lviv, see George Grabowicz, 'Mythologizing Lviv/Lwów: Echoes of Presence and Absence' in John Czaplicka (ed.), Lviv: A City in the Crosscurrents of Culture, Harvard Ukrainian Studies volume XIV (2000), 313-42.

4   Ibid, 41.

5   On Lviv, see Philipp Ther, 'War versus Peace: Interethnic Relations in Lviv during theFirst Half of the Twentieth Century',

6   Ewa Rutkowska, 'Wyznania i narodowości we Lwowie w latach 1857-1939 na tle ogólnej struktury demograficznej miasta' (M.A. diss., Jagiellonian University, Kraków, 1993), 108 and 120.

7   On the role of Lviv as the centre of the Ukrainian national movement in Galicia, see Ivan L. Rudnytsky, 'The Ukrainians in Galicia under Austrian Rule,' in Andrei S. Markovits and Frank E. Sysyn, eds., Nationbuilding and the Politics of Nationalism: Essays on Austrian Galicia (Cambridge, MA, 1983), 38.

8   On the impact of the war on the city, see Henryk Kramarz, Samorząd Lwowa w czasie pierwszej wojny światowej i jego rola w życiu miasta (Kraków, 1994) and Christoph Mich, 'Kriegserfahrung in Lemberg. Vorstellung eines Forschungsprojektes,' in Berichte und Beiträge des Geisterwissenschaftlichen Zentrums Geschichte und Kultur Ostmitteleuropas e.V. 1999 (Leipzig, 1999), 313-30

9   Rutkowska, 'Wyznania i narodowości,' 108-21; On the census of 1931, see also Grzegorz Siudut, 'Pochodzenie wyznaniowo-narodowościowe ludności Malopolski

Wschodniej i Lwowa wedle spisu ludności z 1931 roku,' in Henryk W. Zaliński and Kazimierz Korolczak, eds., Lwów: Miasto, Spoleczeństwo, Kultura. Studia z dziejów Lwowa, vol. 2. (Kraków, 1998),, 271-72 and Piotr Trojański, 'Liczba, rozmieszczenie oraz struktura wewnętrzna 1udności wyznania mojżeszowego w województwie lwowskim w okresie międzywojennym,' in ibid, 254-55.

[10] Statystyka Polski, ser. C (Warsaw, 1938), fasc. 94a.

[11] Rutkowska, 'Wyznania i narodowości,' 123-25.

[12] Marian Tyrowicz, Wspomnienia o życiu kulturalnym i obyczajowym Lwowa: 1918-1939 (Wrocław, 1991), 34; on the migration from Lviv see also Jerzy Holzer, 'Von Orient die Fantasie, und in der Brust der Slawen Feuer...': Jüdisches Leben und Akkulturation im Lemberg des 19. und 20. Jahrhunderts,' in Peter Faßler, Thomas Held, and Dirk Sawitzki, eds., Lemberg, Lwów, Lviv. Eine Stadt im Schnittpunkt europäischer Kulturen (Cologne, 1993), 87.

[13] Pawel Korzcc, 'The Steiger Affair,' Soviet Jewish Affairs 3, no. 2 (1973): 38-57.

[14] BA-MA, RH 28-1/20 and RH 28-1/266 (1. Gebirgsdivision).

[15] An estimate of 2,000 victims over two days can be found in Jacob Gerstenfeld-Maltiel, My Private War: One Man's Struggle to Survive the Soviets and the Nazis (London: Vallentine Mitchell, 1993), p. 54. This estimate was supplied by the Judenrat (Jewish Council), of which Gerstenfeld-Maltiel was an employee. Among the higher estimates is 5,000, in Vasilii Grossman and Il'ia Erenburg (eds.), Chernaia Kniga (Jerusalem, 1980), p. 105.

[16] For detailed Ukrainian police reports of involvement in Aktions, see USHMM, Acc.1995.A.1086, reels 2 and 3.

[17] BA-BL, R 58/214, p. 191, Ereignismeldung UdSSR no. 24, July 16, 1941.

[18] Petliura was in fact assassinated on May 25, 1926, rather than in July. However, perpetrators of the pogrom used the memory of his assassination to incite violence.

[19] P. Friedman, 'The Destruction of the Jews of Lwów,' p. 285.

[20] DALO, R-31/1/1 (Mayoral decree, July 27, 1941).

[21] DALO, R-35/12/50 (Publication of the Judenrat, January 1, 1942); P. Friedman, 'The Destruction of the Jews of Lwów,' pp. 251-57, 296-97; David Kahane, Lvov Ghetto Diary, trans. Jerzy Michalowicz (Amherst, (MA: Univ. of Massachusetts Press, 1990), pp. 13-25. Kahane was a member of the Judenrat's Religious Affairs Department.

[22] USHMM, RG-15.069 (AżIH), 229/3, page 1and following, 229/22, page 3, and 229/53.

[23] Dieter Pohl, Nationalsozialistische Judenverfolgung in Ostgalizien 1941-1944 (Munich, 1996), pp. 159-60. Hans Kujath was the mayor (Stadthauptmann) of Lwów from August 1941 to February 1942. He was succeeded in this position by Egon Höller. District Galicia Governor Karl Lasch was imprisoned and succeeded by Otto Wächter in January 1942.

[24] P. Friedman, 'The Destruction of the Jews of Lwów,' p. 254; Eliiakhu Iones, Evrei L'vova v gody vtoroi mirovoi voiny i katastrofy evropeiskogo evreistva 1939-1944, ed. Svetlana Shenbrunn (Moscow: Rossiiskaia biblioteka Kholokosta, 1999), pp. 134, 140. The historian Iones survived forced labor in Kurowice, outside Lwów.

[25] Sometimes this reprieve meant ultimate survival, as in the case of Rabbi David Kahane. During an Aktion in November 1942, a Jewish policeman who recognized Kahane opened the door to a building (without a bribe) so that the rabbi could hide. See David Kahane, Lvov Ghetto Diary, trans. Jerzy Michalowicz (Amherst, MA: Univ. of Massachusetts Press, 1990), p. 81. On attitudes towards the Jewish police, see P. Friedman, 'The Destruction of the Jews of Lwów,' pp. 254-55.

[26] E. Iones, Evrei L'vova, pp. 144-45.

[27] BA-MA, RH 53-23/33 through RH 53-23/38 (Oberfeldkommandantur 365, monthly reports of the Chief Medical Officer); DALO, R-2042/1/55 (Aktenvermerk, January 10, 1942, regarding postponement of resettlements). On negotiations with Jewish leaders, see P. Friedman, 'The Destruction of the Jews of Lwów,' pp. 263-64, 278-79. Rumors suggested that these negotiations involved bribery.

[28] D. Pohl, Judenverfolgung, p. 199. After the war, Friedrich Katzmann assumed a false identity. He died in Darmstadt, Germany, in 1957. See also Nbg. Doc. 018-L (Katzmann Bericht, June 30, 1943).

[29] P. Friedman, 'The Destruction of the Jews of Lwów,' pp. 270, 277.

[30] Bella Gutterman (ed.), Days of Horror (Tel Aviv: 1991), pp. 203, 210; and D. Pohl, Judenverfolgung, p. 223.

[31] P. Friedman, 'The Destruction of the Jews of Lwów,' pp. 280, 282.

[32] P. Friedman, 'The Destruction of the Jews of Lwów,' p. 273.

[33] BA-MA, RH 53-23/38 (Oberfeldkommandantur 365, September 1942).

[34] Within the labor office, Heinz Weber led the 'Judeneinsatzstelle,' the department that oversaw Jewish labor until its dissolution in August 1942. Jews were employed as staff members in the Judeneinsatzstelle.

[35] USHMM, RG-31.003M, reel 1 (requests from private enterprises for Jewish labor); BA-MA, RH 23/13 (Rüstungskommando Lemberg), and RH 53-23/38-39 (Oberfeldkommandantur 365).

[36] P. Friedman, 'The Destruction of the Jews of Lwów,' p. 295.

[37] P. Friedman, 'The Destruction of the Jews of Lwów,' pp. 286-89. Wilhelm Mansfeld commanded the Julag for the short interval before Josef Grzymek took over. Grzymek received a death sentence in a Polish war crimes trial and died in 1949.

[38] D. Pohl, Judenverfolgung, pp. 258 and following, and 360; P. Friedman, 'The Destruction of the Jews of Lwów,' p. 298; and E. Iones, Evrei L'vova, pp. 202-204, 292.

[39] The historian Philip Friedman, who survived the Holocaust in Lwów, claims to have received this data from the head of the Jewish committee. See Friedman, 'The Destruction of the Jews of Lwów,' 317.

[40] For trials and death sentences of local civilians who hid Jews, see USHMM, Acc.1995.A.1086, reel 29.

[41] For Żegota reports from Lwów, see USHMM, RG-15.070M, reel 4.

[42] Ibid., pp. 284-85 and 295-96; and E. Iones, Evrei L'vova, pp. 286-87.

Part II

OUR PEOPLE

The Wartime Diary

of *Edmund Kessler*

Lwow, Poland
1942–1944

Original Page from Edmund Kessler's Diary

TERROR IN LWOW

The first day passed in relative calm. The German soldiers generally did not assault Jews. But the military police, tall, muscular, well-armed — the embodiment of Prussian Militarism and brutality — sporadically attack innocent Jewish passersby. The conquerors escorted by the Ukrainian rabble, vent their bestiality, making rude jokes, and maltreating those few compelled to leave their homes. These Jews were ordered to bow and take their hats off, and then they were slapped in the face and kicked.

The local Ukrainians, wearing holiday clothes with blue and yellow ribbons — their national colors — pinned on their chests, at first gaze at these vicious games, taken aback by their crudity. To stop an elderly man peacefully walking in the street and then to force him to stand at attention while slamming his face for no reason and without pity, is something one has to learn. A diligent student soon masters the game on his own, his peasant greed bidding him to combine amusement with practicality. What would not be simpler than to seize the opportunity to grab a watch or extract a wallet? After all, the victim is defenseless and there is not even a question of anyone intervening.

The indifference of man to man is beyond belief. Our people are excluded from normal society. Although the majority feel a kind of relief owing to the fact that the bearers of culture from the East [Soviets] are leaving this unfortunate land, still, they are gripped by worry and anxiety over what the next day will bring. The Ukrainian mob, encouraged by the behavior of the Germans, is further prodded by rumors spread about the bestial tortures Jews supposedly inflicted on arrested political prisoners. Anti-Semitic pogroms begin on the first day of their entry in Lwow feel empowered by the new authorities [Nazis][1]

The notoriously low degree of education and intelligence of the Ukrainian masses with their narrow-minded clergy and bourgeoisie, do not prevent the mob, poorly educated and gullible, from assuming the role of judge and jury. Feeling political and moral superiority, it charges the Jews with misdeeds of which they are innocent. The Ukrainian archbishop[2] preaches a sermon in which, instead of calming the excited mood and taming their barbarous instincts, he demagogically incites the mobs, and in the name of their sacred religion, calling upon the population to retaliate against Jews for their supposed bestial murder of political prisoners, even though these prisoners included some Jews too.

The murders are done, but as to who actually committed them, that was a lesser issue. Let the weakest, the most defenseless people be blamed, and they happened to be Jews. This is Judgement Day. Kangaroo-court justice is carried out. The (multi-thousand) judge and jury of the people, many of them drunk, bamboozled by the Germans, shout hoarsely the charges and the verdict, expressing their rage for bloodlust revenge. It would be vain to look for the gravity of a real court of law in this situation. The black wings of the Angel of Death rustle over the stilled, fear-stricken Jewish masses.

The following days bring the verdict of the execution, a verdict pronounced by one community on another, executed [shamelessly] by one mass on another. A fanatic mob orgy of bloodshed and pillage began, but even so it took place according to a certain system. The orchestrators here were the Germans. It is they who decided when to begin the pogrom, when to stop it, how long to torture the victims; whether until they lose consciousness or to slaughter them. They act capriciously toward their Ukrainian subordinates, even beating them when they are slow or overzealous in carrying out orders. They thus emphasize that they are the masters while the native, Ukrainians and the Poles exist merely to carry out their commands.

They organized patrols, each consisting of three or four teenagers and farm laborers from the surrounding villages, which criss-cross the city streets and check the identities of the pedestrians. Anyone who has the misfortune of having "Jew" written on his internal passport is detained, his passport[3] confiscated, and then is promptly escorted to a collection point and beaten. These militiamen are abundantly equipped with torture instruments-iron-shod clubs, sticks, shovels, hammers, hatchets, rubber nightsticks, and knuckle-dusters. These are used to beat victims all over their bodies. The sight of blood does not weaken the lust to kill, on the contrary, it stimulates it. German patrols ensure that the victims do not resist and the torturers do their job properly, not that they lack the desire for it. The public enjoys gaping at this spectacle, at this martyring of innocent people. Rarely does someone cast a disapproving glance at the assassins or reacts with pity or disgust at what transpires. Still, there are instances of individuals who actively defend a publicly beaten and humiliated woman or warn a Jewish passerby against the death waiting for him at the next step. But these are isolated instances. Occasionally, someone loudly protests in defense of the bestially beaten Jews or even puts up an active resistance to the assailants, but he is quickly silenced and called a stooge for the Jews.

The Jews generally behave passively. They let themselves be punched, tortured, and beaten. With a dumb resignation, they submit to terror. From the first day, from the first moment, the victims seem deprived of the will to act, the will to resist. Their faces are contorted in a grimace of despair and sometimes of impotent anger, but mostly reflect resignation. Without delay, they surrender their property to the assaulting militiamen.

At times they try to bribe assailants, but that rarely works. More often, a passport or some receipt issued in German language saves the victim. For the militia, as this band of robbers calls itself, are mostly illiterates, and panic at the sight of any German-language document, especially when it is stamped with the symbol of the German eagle or "the bird." Such a document confers the right of extra-territoriality on the victim and makes its possessor untouchable.

The Jews, who are not told the reason why they are stopped, seek no explanation. They know it is sufficient that they are Jews. While beating them, the militiamen shout that this is revenge for their murdered brothers and sisters (who had really been murdered by the NKVD).

The Jews are ordered to wash corpses. The very thought of it causes the victims to shiver. To touch with one's very hands these corpses is horrible, worse than the physical beatings. They do not realize that "washing the corpses" is moral chicanery, serving to turn them into corpses themselves, as part of an orgy of murder and tortures.

Heavy traffic crowds the streets. Hundreds of troop-carrying vehicles race toward three prison buildings. The faces of civilians and soldiers beam with satisfaction. Nothing can impair the gravity of the moment.

After all, the corpses of the murdered political prisoners are to be identified. Attention is solely focused on the Jews, who, aligned in rows of four, are escorted in the direction of prison buildings. Picked up at collection points or directly wrested from the house doors and streets, they are robbed, beaten, and vilified. But their real tragedy was to transpire shortly.

The chief Rabbi of the city, sensing mounting misfortune from that very morning, puts on his vestments and proceeds to visit the head of the Ukrainian church with a request for help and intervention[4]. He is received coolly and indifferently, although he is linked to the Metropolitan by ties of personal acquaintanceship, and finally departs with an air of resignation. The Metropolitan does not intend to intervene with the authorities in defense of the Jews.

The affair is of a purely political nature; as for its moral and religious aspects, the Metropolitan does not perceive them. In his opinion, the Ukrainian population, because it knows how to retain tact and moderation, cannot be held responsible for the behavior of isolated individuals.

Embittered and resigned, anticipating the worst, the rabbi returns home, pondering the response of the prince of the church. But he has little time left for meditation. He is stopped at the door of his house by militiamen who are waiting for him. Ignoring his priestly vestments, they beat, insult and dishonor him reveling in their acts. They then escort him and a group of Jews in the direction of the central prison.

The Jews, now aligned in ranks, are forced to march to the execution site. But the avengers regard their numbers as insufficient. A furious search of Jewish homes commences. The rioting, ransacking, and plundering grows in strength and intensity. Beaten, whipped, and tortured, the inhabitants are dragged into the streets. Hiding in the cellar or attic mostly does not help. Gangs of Ukrainian children inspect the nooks and crannies of houses and apartments and point out hidden Jews. The violence and fury of the attackers grow. No one is spared.

The march to Golgotha commences. Tattered masses of tortured Jews arrayed in military formation under the supervision of German soldiers, police, and Ukrainian militia are led to the prisons in the sight of crowds lining the streets.

A wave of people surges up the steepled street toward the prison on Lackiego Street, a pitiful procession jeered by the crowds, beaten and driven by the executioners. Little children spit at the sight of the Jews barely dragging themselves, as their elders set the example, as they insult, mock, and hit the victims.

This nightmarish procession is creeping uphill for hours. The victims by now look like ghosts, blood trickling from their wounds. All they lack are crowns of thorns and crosses. They neither beg for mercy from their executioners nor do complain about their fate. Their pain is the pain of the Jewish nation; their blood is its blood. No one suffers individually. Having experienced so much brutality, they have lost the will to resist and the weakest are ready to give up and die. Here and there one can see a tottering old woman or man supported by someone younger. After all, they are forbidden to stop and catch their breath.

An old, exhausted man has suddenly fallen. Blood and foam trickled from his mouth. His pale lips whisper incomprehensible words. The jeering mob quiets for a moment; the procession halts. Those nearest to him try to rescue him, but a German soldier shoots in the direction of those surrounding the old man and beats them with the butt of his rifle while cursing them coarsely.

In a moment the procession resumes walking toward the site of execution. The old man's corpse is flung aside. The mob keeps beating and deriding the victims. The huge prison courtyard is surrounded on all sides with a wooden wall that is more than two meters high on the site of the execution. A wide gate in front of the wall is lined by German guards and on both sides of the gate stand rows of Ukrainians wearing the uniforms of the Soviet militiamen. They are armed with iron-shod sticks and they greet the entering victims with a hail of blows and insults.

The courtyard, thickly ringed with machine guns tended solely by the Germans, is interspersed with soldiers armed with light machine guns, pistols, and grenades who ensure that no one escapes his fate or is spared even the least torture.

Shouts and noise resound throughout the courtyard. The crowds clustered around the gate, which apparently have grown accustomed to the suffocating stench of the executed political prisoners' bodies, hurl curses and stones at each entering group of Jews as these totter under the blows, half-conscious from the rocks thrown at their heads. They move lethargically as if in a dream, without will, under the duress of their torturers.

Without resisting and delaying they carry, from one place to another, the corpses of the murdered political prisoners. Without prodding, they dig graves and wash the corpses. They do not even react when German soldiers strike them with their rifle butts, as dozens of their fellow victims fall and lose consciousness. Their executioners then order them to lift the bodies.

Incessant shooting accompanies these tortures, but the shots no longer terrify the victims. Their only conscious thought and silent prayer is to be struck by a well-aimed bullet that will put an end to their suffering.

The tortures grow more refined, beginning with the digging of graves, while the crowd flings curses and stones at them. The soldiers who supervise this [infernal] activity demand that they use a child's toy shovel or just their bare hands to dig a pit large enough and deep enough for a man to lie down in. If the task is completed on time, the soldiers promise the victim a direct shot in the heart, which excites derisive laughter from the onlookers.

The less inventive German soldiers order the victims to wipe the gunpowder off their boots with their tongues, or to stand for hours facing the wall while the soldiers constantly cock their rifles or shoot point blank at the victims.

Those shot down must be buried in mass graves by their comrades. The victims stand for hours in the summer heat, fainting from hunger and thirst, awaiting their execution as salvation. They mechanically bury those already shot, envying these still warm corpses their martyrdom. They bury the corpses in the ground, covering their graves with just a handful of earth. Some bodies are still quivering and have not yet completely expired their last breath. Their lips have neither uttered the words of the *Viddui*, the Hebrew prayer before dying, nor appealed to God for help, nor called for revenge. The bodies disappear under the earth without a trace or remembrance. No one weeps for them, no one mourns.

The Ukrainian servants of the Germans dishonor these corpses, kick them, and spit on them, but not before searching them thoroughly for anything of value. Despite the duration of the executions, the public's enthusiasm does not wane. The onlookers encourage them with shouts to become even more brutal. What ensues is competition of hitting the victims and kicking the corpses. Their crescendo of curses and shots silence the death rattle of the dying on this devilish day of slaughter.

The Ukrainians compete in devising ever more refined tortures. The German executioners seem to become fed up with the excessive zeal of their assistants and strike them in the face, calling them Ukrainian swine. The newly entered groups of Jews are placed against the wooden fence; they are exhausted by hours of standing in the scorching heat and suffering hunger and thirst while waiting for execution. Some of them faint and fall to the ground. Only the Ukrainian onlookers seem tireless. They regard the tragic sight of the burial of the murdered political prisoners as a Roman gladiatorial game. Eating and drinking, hour after hour, they enjoy the gruesome sight, their thirst for blood unquenchable. Finally, around 8 o'clock, the Germans order the ending of the pogrom. The torturers have exhausted themselves physically, as well as morally.

Local collaborators drive away the surviving Jews of the slaughter and throw the corpses of the martyred victims into the street. The gutters of Kopernika Street brim with corpses, some of them still alive and scarcely breathing. The surviving Jews who can barely stand on their feet try to resuscitate them, in hopes that they will reach their homes before the hour of nine, when no one may be outside on pain of death. In tatters and rags, the victims drag themselves through the darkened streets, resembling ghosts more than humans. Those pedestrians to whom fate has granted a better ethnic origin and did not brand with the stigma of Jewishness, for the most part, walk indifferently past these specters.

THE RETURN HOME

Pain and sorrow are slow to penetrate the consciousness of the martyred victims. As if they turned to stone, they neither talk, nor complain. They fall into silence as if petrified by their pain. Days pass; their wounds begin to heal outwardly. Slowly consciousness returns. They recount their recent experiences in muted voices, now and then stopping as if their words were choking them. At such intervals they weep, seemingly not with tears, but with blood.

In those memorable days similar scenes in two other prisons: at the so-called Brigidka on Kaimierowska Street and at the military prison on Zamarsynowska — places of execution — are not crowded with the select public attracted the day before from the suburbs and villages. There, the executions of the Jews were conducted in prison cells with every possible chicanery. Before being executed, victims had to stand for hours with their arms raised, facing the walls in darkened cells. Their executioners consisting almost exclusively the German police, the Gestapo, and the SS, killed them by machine gun and grenade, preceded by shooting dozens of bullets into the air with victims being forced to look at those already killed. The beaten and whipped Jews from the higher floors of the prison were shoved out of windows. Both Aryan and Jewish eyewitnesses say that they shall not forget until their dying day, the moans of the executed.

The executions continued till late at night, only to cease when the order to stop them came, which clearly surprised the executioners, who regretfully released the survivors of this pogrom, nearly all who suffered broken ribs.

The following is told by a Jew who survived these tortures: "At about ten in the morning, I, together with two rabbis, the brothers Lewin, was led to the prison on Kazimierzowska Street. We were driven with rifle-butt blows into one of the cells and ordered to face the walls with our arms raised. I do not remember how many executioners watched us inside the cell, but I do believe there were several, all Germans.

They told us they would conduct an investigation, which began by asking names and surnames and dates of birth. Our answers were confirmed in the form of a blow in the side with a rifle butt. Anyone who was so stunned by the first blow as to delay giving an answer, was struck again and again until he answered the question.

One of the inquisitors of this system found it too simple. To diversify it, he bade his comrades to strike the detainees in the face as well. After this inquisition, the first ten detainees were told that the investigation produced sufficient grounds for sentencing them to death. Frightened and beaten, we could not believe our own ears. Soon the first ten were escorted out of the cell. A moment later the rat-tat-tat of a machine gun drowned the moans of the dying. Four of the tallest and strongest among us were selected to bury our slaughtered comrades in return for the promise that we would be the last to die. Those who refused to bury their brethren were shot dead on the spot.

When their turn came, both rabbis gave no answers and instead began to recite the prayer before dying, as well as a blessings for us. This infuriated the Germans. These rabbis found the audacity to remain calm in the face of death. The rabbis were beaten and then dragged out of the cell. Soon shots heard from an adjacent cell enabled us to learn what fate they had encountered.

This 'questioning' lasted until late at night. I awakened lying in a street gutter. Some unknown "Aryan" approached me and asked what had happened to me. Seeing that I could not move, he lifted me and carried me home. He did not give me his name or address, saying that after the war we would be, 'in touch'."

The subsequent day which hardly relieved the tension, gave the impression that the pogrom would continue endlessly. In Polish territory occupied by the Soviets there had not been any organized legal representation of the Jewry, which magnified our anxiety. Some had cherished the illusion that setting up such representation would halt the permanent pogrom, only to discover how vain this hope would become later.

Banned from freely moving in the streets, the Jewish population was starved as food shortages arose; much as it had during the first days of the German and Soviet invasion of Poland. Bombings magnified the devastation to buildings caused by the fighting. Industry and trade, concentrated during Soviet times in the hands of state and cooperative organizations, suffered such a powerful shock that several weeks were needed to put the entire machinery back in motion. The mistrust of the Soviet ruble and the relatively weak confidence in the new currency, as well as the uncertainty about the ratio of one to another, further added to the commercial chaos.

In these conditions, Jewish purchase of food on the free market was difficult , and was practically impossible for rationed food in state owned stores for reasons of politics and personal safety.

Hunger pervaded Jewish dwellings. Those lacking contact with the Aryan population or with any considerable domestic food stocks were condemned to starvation. But that was not the greatest misfortune. Far worse was the impossibility of going out into the streets. Patrols organized by newly formed militia hunted Jews in the streets. Regardless of age, gender, condition of health, or education, any Jew encountered was detained and escorted to a collection point or to the Gestapo established power-station building on Pelczynska Street.

Within the next two days 4,000 people were captured, whereupon a selection took place in the power-station building. Artisans and construction workers were assigned for doing various chores for the Gestapo, while the remainder were trucked in the direction of Zimna Woda and Brzuchowice, where they were executed. Hundreds of innocent people were placed in mass graves dug by some of them just before their shooting. Only a few succeeded in escaping the sight of the execution. Their stories of what happened would freeze the blood in the veins. Jews were collected en masse in the courtyard of the building on Pelczynska Street and ringed by machine guns, they were held there for two days under a scorching sun, without food or water while Gestapo men beat them incessantly. Torturing and mistreating people was a source of enjoyment to them.

THE SYSTEMATIC INTIMIDATION
OF OUR PEOPLE

The victims, threatened with being shot, were forced to stand facing the wall for hours, enduring jeering and beatings. One of the fugitives had witnessed the following scene: Some forty Jews, gathered in a large room, were ordered to stand facing the wall. The Gestapo men struck their victims with iron-shod cudgels. Suddenly an officer appeared, looking discontented and satisfied. He assaulted one of the victims with a powerful kick of his boot, whereupon he began a mad dance on the victim's belly, ripping it apart, so that its internal organs were spilling out.

No German officers looking upon this scene protested. No one tried to calm the raging madman. Indeed, everyone seemed gratified to look upon this horrible spectacle.

Those assigned to work were perhaps not treated as brutally: they were forced to clean toilets with the aid of toothbrushes while crawling around on all fours and barking like dogs. One group whose members were ordered to clear a segment of a lawn by tearing out each blade of grass with their teeth, were carefully monitored by their cruel masters, to make sure that they would not even have a moment's rest.

People who were not accustomed to such hard physical labor collapsed physically and mentally. After the first two days, those first selected laborers, were told they would be placed in a barrack or a camp as permanent employees of the Gestapo. What occurred inside to the others will be related later.

After the first few days of terror and mass execution, life began to calm down somewhat, but seizure of people from the streets did not stop. The only difference being that those detained were not executed by shooting but assigned hard physical labor at military bases.

The unlimited demand for manpower was not dictated by military necessity, but rather, by convenience. Jews were made to handle the numerous big and little maintenance chores normally done by the German police and military personnel themselves.

At first, Jews avoided getting dragooned for such labor, fearing chicanery, maltreatment, and beatings, but their enviable status there became the desirable. Even those who had never experienced physical labor before in their lives, now were anxious to do such labor, especially at workplaces managed by the Viennese, for those as a rule treated Jews decently, gave them fair work assignments and often displayed sympathy for their fate.

Thus, this positive attitude toward physical labor imbued Jews with the illusory hope of survival. Nevertheless, the authorities kept treating them with open hostility. A forced labor camp was established by Sokolniki near Lwow. It was managed by Ukrainian sadists who bestially tortured their victims. The victims, forced to do backbreaking field work, were given a daily food ration of watery soup and 100 grams of bread. The days that street razzias were organized to seize more people for the camp, were days of fear for the Jewish population.

The establishment of the Jewish representation, or the Judenrat, in the last days of July 1941, calmed Jewish anxiety somewhat. People thought the authorities had conferred a kind of legal status to the Jewish community with the creation of the Judenrat. It was assumed that this would regulate the now burning issues of Jewish forced labor, camps, food rationing, and housing, which would now receive immediate organizational attention. But the most important and pressing was the problem of employment. The newly established German "labor office" immediately called upon all former government employees to return to their Soviet-era posts, an impossibility for Jews who faced the danger of being seized for forced labor on the way to or from work. Moreover, officials recruited from among the Ukrainians to administer former Soviet institutions, fired Jews en masse, who were refused employment cards. Within several weeks, Jewish white-collar workers were completely eliminated from the local economy.

The number of blue-collar workers also declined markedly. Many Jews were forced into military and civilian labor. Socio-economic changes which normally would have taken years, occurred within a short time. Academics, scholars, individuals in the free professions, who had until then worked with their minds using pen and paper, now wielded shovels and picks, having to adapt themselves to the changed conditions of life.

These radical changes sometimes elicited respect among even the greatest enemies of the Jews. Owing to the terror and violence, the Jewish masses rapidly became proletarians in their efforts to keep the Jewish community alive. The slogan of making the Jewish masses productive was translated into reality so as to rebut their foes' accusation that Jews are an antisocial unproductive element.

The Judenrat set up a labor office in order to provide German workplaces with the laborers they needed. Only then did the plague of raids slowly diminish.

THE JUDENRAT

The German Police and political authorities established the Judenrat rather arbitrarily, selecting a variety of individuals and professionals who had little in common with the living organism of the Jewish community itself other than being Jewish too. Some of them were completely asocial or assimilated to such a degree that they had completely lost contact with the Jews. These included disgraced politicians and other disreputable individuals who, emulating their barbarous masters, tried to exercise dictatorial power over the drowning Jewish masses; it included people whom the Jewish community had long since excluded owing to their total lack of personal and social ethics, not to mention the dregs of society whom the tide of Jewish misfortune raised to the surface like muck after a flood. Others still completely unknown to the community owed their distinction to personal contacts with underground Ukrainian elements operating covertly in Soviet times[5].

The future of the Jews now lay in the hands of this motley group. The first task on behalf of the German authorities, all to be achieved within a very short period of time — five days, was to exact a levy of 20 million rubles from the community. That was not a difficult task, for the Jewish community rose immediately to the occasion, surrendering even more than the specified amount. The most victimized, the gray mass of people who had already been proletarianized, rendered paupers by the Bolshevik occupation and robbery of their assets, contributed the most, while rich Jewish bourgeoisie and the intelligentsia remained, on the whole, aloof.

More than once the Judenrat had to mobilize all its resources, using publicity to persuade people who could but would not contribute to the levy in proportion to their assets, while other less wealthy Jews sacrificed everything, bringing their last candlesticks or wedding rings, or selling for mere pennies their last blankets or pillows. The authorities meanwhile smirked at the broad masses of the Jews agitatedly lining up in front of contribution points and tensely followed the progress of the levy drive.

Anxiety gripped the community as it recalled the initial pogroms costing the lives of about 10,000 people in Lwow. Failure to pay the levy, it was feared, would lead to another pogrom, which the Germans were anyway clearly threatening, an anxiety further stoked by the Judenrat, which at hourly intervals notified the Jewish street that the contributions were still several million short. Some shady individuals had the insolence to set up checkpoints for receiving valuables — clothing, bedding, jewelry — for their personal benefit, were later liquidated with the help of the newly organized Jewish militia.

It would be difficult to say how the non-Jewish population of the city regarded this operation. There were instances of contributions offered by Poles as well anonymous contributions. A mood of cynical gratification, and at best indifference, prevailed among the broad mass of Ukrainians.

The imposition and collection of contributions were preceded by the deplorable incidents on the so-called Petlura Day, the anniversary of Sholom Schwartzbard's[6] heroic assassination in Paris of Hetman Petlura, whose armed forces had slaughtered thousands of Jews in the Ukraine.

The Ukrainian clergy and bourgeoisie utilized this anniversary to again incite the masses against the defenseless Jewish community. Under the supervision by the German Sicherheitpolizei (Security

Police) and the Ukrainian militia, criminal elements rushed in to kill and rob the Jews, thousands of whom were severely beaten and their dwellings ransacked. Lastly, to crown this affair, about 2,000 persons were detained, mostly members of the rich Jewish bourgeoisie and the intelligentsia. On that memorable day most of the Jewish intelligentsia were murdered. From the windows one could see horrible sights: Groups of teenagers armed with cudgels, knives, and shovels rampaged through the half-deserted streets, hitting indiscriminately any passerby who looked Jewish. Thousands of dwellings in the Jewish quarter were plundered and destroyed.

That was an unforgettable day of bloodshed for the Jewish population. In addition to the killed and wounded, some 2,000 persons were taken to an unknown destination. To magnify the horror, nearly all the Jewish synagogues were burned down in the presence of the fire brigades which made sure that the conflagration did not spread to other buildings. Detachments of the SS and police planted explosive charges under the magnificent edifice of the synagogue on Poranska Street, the five-centuries-old landmark on Sobieskego Street, and other temples in the city. The Jews, sad-eyed and full of tears, looked on from the windows of the surrounding buildings, as the flames consumed these ancient buildings together with their decorations and sacred relics.

The barbaric destruction of architectural and cultural landmarks, mostly Jewish temples but also some Catholic churches continued. Attempts to rescue relics sacred not only to Judaism but to Christianity, as well, usually resulted in the rescuers being thrown alive into the flames.

According to many eyewitnesses, some individuals, heedless of the danger, entered the burning synagogues to rescue the Torahs, the most sacred of relics, despite being shot at by the police and, in the end, perishing in the flames. How this affected the Jews is difficult to describe. Thousands orphaned and widowed that day were in the grip of impotent despair. The brutal destruction of holy relics left no doubt that an enemy capable of such sacrilege would draw back at nothing in order to destroy the Jews.

The conditions in Little Poland* made it easier for the foe to accomplish his objectives. People began to realize that the enemy has declared an unconditional war of extinction on the defenseless Jewish masses and, as a result, their total extermination. What resistance, after all, could be put up by a people who were unprepared to fight and to whose mindset the idea of armed struggle was completely alien? Deprived of the great leaders which they needed in those tragic moments, the Jews could only be defenseless fodder to the foe.

Under these circumstances, the news of the compulsory levy prompted a welcome relief and the hope that it would heal the wounds suffered, that the 2,000 arrested on Petlura Day would be freed, and that in general the Germans could be negotiated with by means of money. It was hoped that such concessions would succeed in ensuring the survival of the Jews until the end of the war and prevent a repetition of such great bloodletting as had taken place in the early days.

This basically unsound idea of corrupting the German authorities was taken up by the Judenrat, which persuaded itself and the community that this was the right road. Their strong survival instinct, their faith in life, prompted the Jews to pursue this idea, as if grasping at a life-saving belt. This, as further happenings showed, was the road to perdition. Despite numerous disappointments, until the last moments of their well-nigh total extermination, the Jews clung to this illusion.

Posters affixed to walls declared that the Jewish population irreproachably fulfilled its obligation to pay the levy, but that tribute changed nothing. Those detained on Petlura Day did not return to their homes. The financial sacrifice was for nought. The authorities had deluded the community into believing that now peace would reign, that it now

---

* *Malopolska* or Lesser Poland was part of the Galician Austrian province between 1795–1914. In 1918 it became part of the Second Polish Republic and included Lwow — the former Lemberg.

would be left alone within some framework of legalistic order, despite terrorizing orders of the German authorities, a mistaken conviction in the inveterate legalistic attitude of a supposedly cultured people like the Germans. It was believed that the terror would be confined within some kind of rule of law, so characteristic of the Germans. Soon, too, the first orders of this kind were issued, including the determination of who was a Jew, introducing the stigma of wearing armbands emblazoned with the Star of David.

Anyone who had two Jewish grandparents (regardless of the religion he professed) was determined to be a Jew. An Aryan with no Jewish grandparents who remained married to a Jewish spouse, was considered as belonging to the Kehillah, the Jewish community organization. At the same time, those classified as Jews were ordered to wear white armbands with the Star of David sewn or painted on them in blue; branding them as Jews.

This order caused a deep feeling of humiliation. Assimilated Jews who had until then not stood out from their surroundings in dress and customs, now felt singled out and made to feel more alienated and uncomfortable in an already hostile environment.

Previously scattered among the native population, the Jews were forced by various sanctions to move to the predominantly Jewish quarter of the city. Their Aryan neighbors grew even more alienated from them owing to the introduction of the armbands, and more hostile owing to Nazi sanctions and propaganda. Those who had previously been in cordial and close contacts with Jews or linked to them by ties of friendship, kinship or gratitude, suddenly began to act like strangers and seemed not to recognize them.

People who had in time completely lost contact with the Jewish community and had converted to Christianity, became absorbed in the larger community, while those completely unaware of their Jewish origin suddenly found themselves part of the defenseless Jewish population. Even some Catholic priests in black frocks now wore the Jewish armband.

Although these were isolated instances, the general abyss between the Jews and non-Jews grew ever deeper. Two separate worlds arose. This chasm was deepened by the application of the Nuremberg laws in their entirety and by regulations banning Jews from hiring non-Jewish employees as well as banning trade with Jews and cohabitation with Jews in the same dwelling.

As time went on, the consistent herding together of Jews into the so-called Jewish Residential District, or ghetto, gave rise to a discrete world separated first by mental and then by physical barriers from the so-called Aryan world. The expulsion to the ghetto, be it individually or in groups, was conducted in an extremely ruthless manner.

At first the police and later the housing functionaries handled these expulsions which were cruel and ruthless. The police appeared often unexpectedly, ordering Jewish dwellers to depart at once or soon after. Instances of a grace period of several days were rare. Under the new laws the expellees had the right to take along all their personal property and needed furniture, but in practice they were only allowed to take along the clothing they could wear and the possessions they could carry. Jeered, cursed and often beaten, people packed whatever they could carry, only to find themselves literally on the street.

Finding a place to live in the Jewish Quarter was no simple matter. Those with neither money nor relatives wandered through the streets, now and then being allowed by good-hearted people to stay overnight in their homes.

The Judenrat proved powerless from the start in the face of this tragedy. Lacking competence and strong leadership, it could not force those fortunate enough to already have their homes in this quarter, arbitrarily and groundlessly designated as Jewish, to offer a sleeping place to their homeless and unfortunate brethren.

The ensuing chaos was huge. The continuing inflow of newcomers made it impossible to either keep statistics or develop a realistic settlement plan. Those who had been actively organizing life in the Jewish quarter gave up and disappeared — no one knew where. The days of mass terror were followed by days of mass chaos.

The housing shortage grew abysmal. People who had until recently lived in large houses or luxury apartments now had to accommodate themselves to miserable nooks in cramped dirty and dark hovels lacking sewage facilities.

Food soon became problematic. Initially, before the establishment of the ghetto, the city's rationed food store policy varied. Some stores did not sell anything to Jews while others required them to wait in line for entire days in order to receive a bread ration which at first amounted to 1,500 grams weekly but later dwindled to 525 grams.

To complicate the food supply for the Jews, they were made to stand in a separate queue from that of "Aryans," a decision enthusiastically welcomed by the "Aryan" population, because it received priority of purchase. By the time the Jews were accommodated, little or nothing remained for them.

To further compound their misery, Jews were permitted to make food purchases in stores and marketplaces only at lunch time or between 2PM and 4 PM, a terribly short interval that the German authorities utilized in raiding and seizing Jews for forced labor. As if touched by a magic wand, the lengthy queues in front of the food stores would suddenly scatter upon the appearance of the Ukrainian militia or Germans. Starving and exhausted, the trapped Jews, both men and women, would be driven for forced labor that sometimes continued until late at night.

It took only a month after the entry of the German troops for the issuance of rationed food to be regulated. The Ukrainian cooperative, granted monopoly on selling rationed food opened separate stores for the Jewish population, which admittedly made it possible for them to make modest purchases, only half as large as in the rations for the "Aryans," but apparently that had to suffice.

The same picture prevailed in the free markets. Jews were at first allowed to shop there but only in the afternoon hours, that is, when only spoiled or discarded food was left. The vendors exploited this opportunity by charging horrendous prices or bartering food for goods that were worth much more. The Jews had no choice but to give in to the demands and escape starvation at the price of one's last suit or piece of furniture. Jewish property, hard-earned in the sweat of one's lifelong toil or even in the toil of generations, was transferred to the environs of the city and surrounding villages.

To add insult to injury, this infliction was utilized to further propaganda that Jews were to be blamed for the rise in food prices, when in fact those making this propaganda were themselves responsible for the causes of rising prices. People responded willingly to this anti-Semitic propaganda, either unwittingly or by being partially unaware of the economic causes. Many consciously partook in this exploitation in order to enrich themselves.

Following the organization of the Judenrat and its "executive branch" in the form of the Jewish militia, the German authorities started to establish separate housing area for the Jewish population, which was territorially large, comprising about one-fourth of the city. To be sure, it was dilapidated, the worst part of the city, poorly built up, with 60 percent of it lacking electricity and sewerage pipes. More than 100,000 Jews of Lwow were to be isolated there.[7]

The German order, which vaguely defined the allocation of certain areas for the Jewish quarter, was a harbinger of subsequent orders similarly formulated, such as the creation of two so-called "pre-bridge" areas of settlement, whose purpose was to sow uncertainty and fear among the Jews. It was said that the buildings equipped with such amenities as plumbing were to be set aside for so-called working Jews and artisan Jews. All the other Jews were to be housed elsewhere in the hovels, in the so-called "post-bridge" district.[8]

In fact, however, the Lwow authorities never seriously considered the idea of setting up a Jewish ghetto. Their frequent decisions to include or exclude some or other areas demonstrated that their sole purpose was to concentrate the Jewish population in one place in order to keep it under tighter control. At the same time, the constant movements of the population from one area to another were intended to uncover or destroy the remaining assets of the Jews. The manner in which the authorities ordered and supervised these migrations indicates how important this goal was to them.

In the first half of November 1941, a public ordinance establishing the so-called Jewish Residential District provided a by then "legal" relocation drive commencing on November 12th and ending on November 14, 1941. Jews living on Zolkiewska Street and behind the bridge, were the first to be affected by this unfortunate ordinance, and had to move out within three days. Due to this unpleasant surprise, the area that had been 95 percent inhabited by Jews, who thought it would be part of the ghetto, now had to suffer considerable personal material losses. At the same time, the SS, Gestapo, Security Police, and Ukrainian militia guards were posted on all the five bridges. These so-called bridge guards stayed at their posts until mid-December, that is for more than a month, terrifying the 100,000 Lwow Jews. Armed with machine guns and firearms, they vied in acts of individual and mass terror against the Jews crossing the bridges. Five bridges on Zolkiewska, Zamarstynowska, Peltewna, Zrodlana, and Warsawska Streets were erected as torturing and killing sheds for those unlucky enough to be detained. The worst of these was on the Peltewna Street bridge.

It is difficult to determine the official purpose of these guards. Were they posted to control the transfer of Jewish property to the ghetto, or the harass elderly Jews? At any rate, they accomplished both objectives.

A new ransom of 5 million rubles was levied on the Jewish community to supposedly defray the cost of relocation. This further complicated the situation and caused even greater confusion and terror among the Jews. Additionally, the community was ordered to provide 1,000 men for forced labor in the camp on Janowska Street.

It is difficult to put into words these terrible blows Jews suffered as a whole. The Judenrat used another ransom demand from the them, with scarred blackened eyes. Often, one of the eyes was gouged out or the ear yellowed and the scalp bloody. The few who recovered and retained soundness of mind after that bloodbath whispered painfully through tears about the terrible beatings, mistreatment, and taunts which the victims had to endure before having to undress and being thrown naked into the trucks.

At the site of execution, the procedure was brief. The naked condemned were driven with whips, shot down en masse with machine guns, and buried on the spot in mass graves, which were later presumably exhumed to obliterate the traces of the crime. Indeed, during the period of final extermination of the Jews in the summer of 1943, the remains were dug up and burned.

Top administrative heads of the district openly supervised this infernal conduct. The governor and mayor had very frequently paid an official visit, to the bridge guards and checkpoints, looking on contentedly at the bestial slaughter being carried out by their subordinates. No one among the local population observing these barbarities was moved by the sight of the naked and defenseless old Jewish people being driven in open trucks to the site of execution on freezing days in November and December.

LIFE IN THE CAMPS

At the same time, the bridge guards conducted a new *Aktion*, to fill the camps. Those without labor cards or whose age and appearance prevented inclusion among the old people were taken to the forced labor camps as they were euphemistically called. In fact, they were simply places for torturing, tormenting, and finally executing Jews. Those brutalized at the collection points by the bridge guards were then taken to the camps, from which hardly anyone returned alive. The few exceptions were those who could afford a sizable ransom. After several days in such a camp, once healthy, fit individuals looked like ghosts of themselves: their bodies were bruised, eyes bloodshot, faces wrinkled, legs swollen — phantoms wearing shreds of soiled clothing. A painted brown stripe running down the back of their jackets identified them as camp inmates.

The living conditions of these unfortunates who wore no Star-of-David armbands were extremely primitive. They slept on wooden boards without even straw mattresses. A barrack hut designed for forty persons held 150-200 people. Lice and bugs soon became a horrible plague. Inmates could not own anything other than what they were wearing. The same underclothes hung on their bodies all the time. Only those who had families could put on clean clothing on their way to work. The other unfortunates had to shiver in the cold for hours while their clothing were being washed or deloused during the memorably harsh winter of 1941/42.

Inside the unheated barracks the temperature equaled that outside. Anyway, rarely did the SS guards charged with overseeing the camp, allow the inmates to stay inside during the washing and disinfection of clothing. Those whom the lice and typhus did not kill, those who survived the beatings by the guards, met their death by catching pneumonia. The death of the fevered inmates was hastened by requiring them to appear outside whereupon they were greeted with a stream of ice cold water. Their comrades in misfortune were required by the SS torturers to scrub the sick with rough floor brushes. No one returned alive from such a bath and scrubbing, and after it, only the cemetery awaited.

All this was a game, mere entertainment, compared with what happened every evening after the inmates returned from work and stood in rows for evening roll-call while the camp director verified their names from a list and called out specified punishments. These roll-calls lasted mostly five or six hours, shortening the inmates' sleep to four or five hours daily. After an arduous day of working for 12 hours from six in the morning till six in the evening — the inmates stood at attention for several hours. Anyone whose legs gave way or whom the cold froze, no longer returned to the barracks and received a well-aimed shot in the nape, the notorious so-called *Genickschuss*[9], which ended his life.

An inspection and the dreaded selection of inmates became part of the roll call. The SS executioners selected the sick and those unable to work and then executed them to the sound of music played by the newly created camp orchestra. Mostly gay tunes and melodies served as background music to the shooting of dozens of inmates who were first required to do gymnastic exercises. Illuminated by klieg lights, the inmates were made to run and march, sometimes for as long as two or three hours. Anyone who failed to keep in step with the music, who slowed down, or had a tin ear was killed point blank.

The inmates marched like passive machine-like mannequins, deprived of will. No one put up any resistance, or protested by word or otherwise seemed perturbed by the ongoing orgy of bloodshed. For these were no longer people but ghosts, to whom death appeared as a benevolent liberator. The insolent cynicism, taunts, and jeers of the executioners made no impression on them. They submitted lethargically to the torments inflicted on them, walking in a mystical stupor to meet liberating death.

Their executioners included some 'refined' beasts who, on selecting their victims, assured them that they would not be rough, that the death encountered would be light and easy. And indeed, their shots were well-aimed, their victims dying instantly. These unfortunates had already long before dying lost their minds and reason anyhow. The others, the onlookers, behaved calmly and coldly. They had stared death in the eye all too often to feel any emotion. Besides, to those about to die, death was sheer liberation; releasing them from their bitter sufferings.

Were the victims able to distinguish between good and evil when they experienced unprecedented misfortune? How can comparisons be made in terms of cause and effect when the blackest of nightmares overwhelms and suppresses the instincts of self-preservation. Once bereft of the will to live, they moved like souless mechanisms, constantly sleepy and hungry, ever starving and fearful, ever waiting for liberating death. The food they received could not keep them alive long. In the morning they got a kind of black liquid and 75 grams of bread, baked from bean leavings and barley; at noon some dirty liquid called soup, which lacked any fat or vegetables; and in the evening, again 75 grams of bread and the unsweetened black liquid called "coffee."

It is not surprising that that in these conditions 90 percent of the camp inmates had their limbs swollen with edema. Such nourishment made them listless and sluggish. Under these camp conditions they died in large numbers.

Organized assistance from the Jewish community could not alleviate this misery even a bit. Bribes flowed through the pockets of the camp directors, masters of life and death who unscrupulously pocketed them and carried on as before, as if nothing had happened. No one dared to protest. Those Jews who had access to liaisons with the Judenrat felt fortunate if these directors, mostly SS noncoms or officers, accepted material or financial contributions without inflicting harm on the messengers, contributions which, however large, had no effect on the plight of the inmates.

When the inmates succumbed to physical or mental exhaustion, a bullet was a welcome end. The only other salvation lay in escape, a not merely difficult but impossible proposition, as the fugitive's immediate family and co-workers were held responsible. His family would be transported to the camp and a dozen or so co-workers from his brigade would be executed. Under these circumstances few inmates tried to escape.

In the first stage of its existence, the Lwow camp already contained a sizeable population of 5,000 seized in raids during the establishment of the Ghetto in November and December 1941.

THE GHETTO

These abysmal conditions marked the relocation of the ghetto. To induce a mood of panic, the bridge guards on Pelczynska Street set up an additional check point to which mostly young women were brought. Under the pretext of searching them for jewelry, hard currency, and gold, they were whipped, forced to totally disrobe, and sadistically violated, struck, and kicked. This torture was abetted with the aid of a half crazed Jewish woman who vented her animosity toward women of the intelligentsia by treating them with exceptional brutality, inciting her German superiors to even greater sadism.

The abused women were then trucked to the Lyczakow sands and machine-gunned. House-to-house searches were carried out at night. Exploiting Jews' lack of legal protection, every German soldier felt empowered to search, or rather, plunder their dwellings. No one objected or did anything to stop this. The Ukrainian militiamen on duty felt they lacked the competence to do so, and besides abetted and competed with the soldiers in plundering Jewish property, and in the process enriched themselves at every opportunity.

On the merest pretext of arresting Jews or even on none at all, soldiers barged into Jewish dwellings, seizing whatever they wanted. Threatening the Jews with revolvers (which they often used anyway), they extorted money, hard currency, and jewelry. Organized gangs of soldiers plagued the Jewish quarter at night, forced open the doors of building and homes and plundered their contents, Whoever dared to refuse opening his door paid for it with his life. Often, under the protection of the night, the soldiers dragged their victims outside onto trucks, drove them out of the city, and murdered them.

Lawlessness and brute force reigned on Jewish streets. At gunpoint, victims were forced to reveal the names and addresses of wealthy Jews who would then be robbed. Anyone courageous enough to refuse to give out information or gave false information, also paid for it with his life. Criminal elements and the Ukrainian militia eased the soldiers' plundering by pointing out who the wealthy Jews were or by participating directly in these activities.

The Gestapo authorities and police looked on passively or were actively satisfied by these crimes of the "most honest army in the world." Their behavior, in fact, encouraged this behavior in the troops, while gangs of thieves entered into competition with them, at which point the Gestapo pursued them and finally, after a long period, ended these activities.

The relocation of about 80,000 Jewish families began. About 20,000 "Aryans" living in that quarter were to move out in return. These mass movements were preceded by a frenzied search for dwelling space. In theory, the Housing Office established by the Judenrat handled housing permit allocations; however, it proved unable to cope with its task for no time was left to prepare for resettlement, take stock of available housing or solve the problem of accommodating the resettling of Jews in the dwellings of Jewish families already living in the quarter.

The order to establish the ghetto was sudden, and the deadline for implementing it was short, only four weeks.

In this situation, the Judenrat's Housing Department, itself located in one of the synagogues, could not cope with an avalanche of tens of thousands of applicants for housing assistance. A mass of people suddenly found themselves without a roof over their heads, packed the little synagogue looking for help from those who were unable to give it.

In this chaos, ungovernable crowds of people carried the remains of their miserable possessions; laundry sacks filled with bedding and pots and pans. They filled the street and narrow alleys in front of the Housing Department. Like camping gypsies, they clustered at nearby house doors and in courtyards.

Realizing the impotence of the housing officials, the suddenly homeless somehow tried to cope on their own. They wandered in the vicinity of the bridges in search of a resting place, heedless of the danger lurking there.

The original non-Jewish dwellers of the district, who had to move out of the ghetto, exploited the situation. They demanded and received stupendous sums for the transfer of their homes. The Jews were impotent in the face of such demands. The winter, a severe one, was coming. A place for shelter had to be found. Thus, began the wanderings of the outlawed. An endless line of two-wheeled carts heaped with all kinds of possessions snaked in the direction of the bridges. Before, on, and past the bridges, teenage hoodlums were encouraged by the example of their elders, exploiting the fact that the half-dead terrified Jews were crossing a bridge, especially at dusk, were largely defenseless. The teenage hoodlums launched mass attacks on the Jews, grabbing their possessions or extorting ransoms. Despite these chicaneries, the columns of carts and people continued moving daily toward the Jewish quarter. In front of the bridges one-half of the contents of the carts was confiscated. Ignoring the permits issued by the Mayor of Lwow, these robberies took place openly, day and night. Everything was taken — furniture, food and fuel.

For the entire month until mid-December this forced relocation; unprecedented in the history of civilized Europe, took place under the new order. Many gentiles attracted by the opportunities for easy legalized plunder tolerated by the authorities, flocked under the bridges to shower the tragic procession of Jews toward the ghetto with curses and jeers. It is impossible to estimate how many thousands of Jews were unable to cross the threshold of the ghetto; for even before then thousands of the elderly and sick had fallen victim to their tormentors, while thousands of young men and boys were taken to camps.

Before the Lwow Jews had a chance to recuperate from these losses, before they could dry their eyes from mourning, for those who had been unable to cross the bridges, a new wave of terror began.

Day after day, German vehicles drove through the streets of the ghetto before and past the bridges, requisitioning pots, pans, cutlery, clothing, bedding, and even furniture for military outposts. The owners of all these possessions were treated as if they did not exist and their belongings were free for the taking. Their pots and pans were grabbed directly from the kitchens after spilling their contents on the ground. The bedding was seized without regard to leaving anything for the owners to cover themselves with. Pleading entreaties were met with derisions and protests with beatings and tortures. The elegantly uniformed German officers vied with each other in brutality and rudeness, giving their subordinates an example on how to conduct themselves against the defenseless Jewish population.

The police and Gestapo, making unannounced visits day and night to the wealthier citizens in search of hard currencies and jewelry, committed unimaginable horrors. Families ordered to stay in one of the rooms were subjected to a thorough body search accompanied by inhuman beatings to wrest information on the hiding places of valuables. After this terrible prelude, the search commenced: clothing and bedding were ripped apart, floor boards torn up.

If the search resulted in finding some valuables, their owner was taken away. If the search proved unproductive, a summons to report to the Gestapo came a day or two later. Whoever did not have enough money to sizably bribe the Gestapo, did not return home alive from the cellars on Lackiego Street.

On the Jewish streets hunger, privation, lice, and typhoid fever decimated the population. Forty people died daily of natural causes, tenfold as many as before the war. Cramped housing allowed a maximum dwelling space of barely two square meters per inhabitant. The severe winter of 1941/42 worsened Lwow Jewry's horrible struggle against death.

In these abnormal conditions the Lwow Jews were doomed. But the survival instinct, the desire to endure the misfortune, prevailed in the Jewish masses

REFLECTIONS

The Poetry and Prose of Edmund Kessler, 1942-1944

LWOW BECOMES GERMAN

NUR FUER DEUTSCHE — FOR GERMANS ONLY

Wherever you go or jump nowadays,
You will always see the same sign: *Nur fuer Deutsche.*
Wherever you go,
Paradise is off limits.
Whether to a cinema or to a trolley,
Theatre or a train,
Restaurant or a coffeehouse,
Ordinary tavern or an inn,
Public baths or Turkish baths
To buy something cheaply
To have your shoes repaired,
To attend a ball,
To buy a bouquet of lilies of the valley,
Or shop at a deli store
Or even enter a restroom,
All are closed to you.
Facing this sinister proscription,
Which seems to be everywhere.
You feel furious and outraged,
And ask God the father,
"Have you created the world *Nur fuer Deutsche?* "

Even if you finally finish your studies
And earn a diploma,
Open a licensed engineers office,
You'll be humiliated soon
Because only a German
May bear an engineer's title,
And you'll ask God the Father
Whether He created the world *Nur fuer Deutsche?*
And this question enervates you all the time,
Whether the world is only for the Germans.

When you are young and gifted,
And thirsty for higher knowledge,
The university is closed to you.
If you are not German, you are an outcast!
It is enough to retrain you
In some craft or manual skill,
So thinks our oppressor
That the world is made only for the German.
So claims the horrible Hitler youth, saying
That the Jews must be totally exterminated.
Morality and Law do not count…
At that time we were still three million…
Some reacted with outrage. Refusing to tolerate
                                    such atrocities
But the soldiers did not care and began killing the Jews.

We who have survived thus far
Oppose these empty protests.
From the voices of the condemned:
"The world should be seated on the bench
                                    of the accused!"

THE LEVY

There was one levy, then another, so many
I no longer remember what they were for.
As soon as the Germans entered Lwow,
they imposed the first levy on us.
Even earlier they rounded up several thousand Jews.
Maybe ten thousand or more.
The detainees were to be released on payment
                                                    of the first levy.
What crock! How easily we were fooled!
We paid the first levy with zeal and eagerness,
The wealthy gave pennies, the poor gave all,
Contributing whatever money they had.
To ransom their poor brothers.
Then suddenly the ominous news broke:
Not enough money was collected to pay the levy.
Instead, gold and silver would be accepted.
The Jews sacrificed their valuables,
One brought a gold necklace, another a set of tableware,
And still another, a candlestick, or coffee cups.
Of the numerous willing contributors
the wealthy gave only grudgingly.
To ransom lives
Is praised by the Holy Scripture, which notes,
That he who demands ransom is beyond redemption
And nothing can save his soul.
To save himself every person
Must pay the required 18 zlotys.

On the day Levy was paid, it was celebrated.
Thereby, it was thought that the Jews
Would be saved from the Jaws of death.
But death is incorruptible.
It does not accept bribes.
Its power is absolute.
The Jews were under watch.
More orders were issued.
Countless
And ever more grasping Fulfilled without protesting
In the belief that their lives would be saved.

DEATH IS INCORRUPTIBLE

Another pause, but not for long
They briskly returned and began another roundup
And we knew our time had come
At first several Jews were taken from their homes
Perhaps ten or more
We thought the first to be captured would be spared
How naïve we were. They were slaughtered
                            with zealous delight
Some begged the small-souled executioners for life
But they refused to listen
Other Jews offered to ransom their brethren
At a certain moment, in the burning sun
The news spread that more money was needed.
Lacking the cash for ransom
They surrendered jewelry of silver and gold
Which the hands of their fathers had fashioned.
One man brought candlesticks
Another all of his jewelry
Still another his new suit
Sacrifices to the golden calf
Those who had nothing to offer trembled with fear.
He who refuses to sacrifice,
To save the people,
Nothing will help him…

The day on which the levy was paid
Was celebrated solemnly

Surely the people were redeemed from
                                    the claws of death
But death is incorruptible.

All across the city on the Prussian wall posters
Goebbles hurls insults in our faces
Everywhere you behold the Prussians
Strange and different,
With needle-sharp eyes and thin noses
Sly brutish faces.
In trim uniforms And hobnailed boots,
                                    for these Spartans
The slogan,
Today Europe and tomorrow the world!
You look at these figures and wonder,
Are these Supermen? But no, I see only
Superthugs, and I despair at this horrible world
In which people like Goebbels and his
                                    German Reich exist.

WILL THIS MAN BE MERCIFUL?

Will this man be merciful?
He shall rather persecute you
Intoxicated with faith in his deeds

God must feel outraged.
And you shall ask the Lord,
Have you created the world "Nur fuer Deutsche?"
When you finally created the world
And completed it with a diploma
You surely did not know what you would be creating
And you soon feel chagrined
By your diploma, O Lord
You think this may be a dream
And you shall ask the Lord
If he created the world "Nur fuer Deutsche"
Your thoughts drain the brain
Has this [morally] crippled nation crossed the line?
In its desire for power
Its road to heaven is barred
For this nation
Is unaware of being damned.

THE LWOW GHETTO

THE GHETTO IS BURNING

The Flames Spread

The ghetto, the Lwow Ghetto, is burning.[10]
Our people drowning in rivers of blood.
Our blood is streaming in the gutters,
Blood gushing from the mouths and ears of the victims,
Blood which the earth has massively absorbed,
Blood which fertilizes the earth.
Golden sheaves of flames rise to the skies.
The azure blue of the heavens turns red
The earth joins with the sky in a sea of fire and blood.
Patrols stand on a little square in the city.
Where commanders receive reports.
Lines of luxurious cars.
Young officers directing engaged in the *Aktion*
Holding submachine guns, elegantly uniformed,
Issue terse orders that no one has considered
And that quickly, thoughtlessly, decide the lives
                               of thousands.
The more corpses the better. Executing their duties
                     with pleasure and enthusiasm,
Gripped by a raging bloodlust.
A big barrel of alcohol stokes their rage, threatening
                           loss of reason

All are insanely drunk. All delight in carrying
                              out horrible atrocities.
Crazed with rage, they beat and shoot people
And sometimes even hang them.
Gladdening their hearts.
Their faces are aglow with zeal
After all, they are famous all over
the world for their stout hearts and barbarism.

In the center of the little square lit bonfires
Illuminate moaning wounded burning Jews.
From the hellish fires
Their cries rise to the sky.
Those still living writhe in smoke
In this spectacle within a dense cloud, people
                              and nature die, drown, disappear.
Now and then a messenger rushes in as if from
                              a battlefield.
Taking a swallow of the potent drink from the barrel,
He proudly reports thousands of Jews are dying
                              in his sector,
How many are being tortured to death, in what sector,
And how bravely the young SS men perform their duties
Spewing a hurricane of death from the barrels
                              of their weapons
At men, women, and children. Now
Attempts are made to conserve ammunition
And shoot only when absolutely necessary.
                              The heads of little
Children smashed against the wall burst open
                              like poppy pods.
He recalls humorously how he met
                              a little funny Jewish boy

And ordered him to stand against the wall.
The boy asked him several times, like a fool,
Just where he was expected to stand.
He acted as if he did not understand his fate.
Though his voice sounded choked, when he was shot,
                          he did not even bat an eyelid.
The messenger's tale triggered a burst of laughter among
The listeners who praised him called him a great guy.
After all, the murderer was big and the boy was little.
A brief conference was held afterward,
All agreed that every Jewish child would
Meet the somber fate of having its little head smashed
Against the wall.
In return, the executioners would be thanked
                          by the Fuehrer
For saving bullets when killing little Jews.

In a moment the messenger rushes in,
Bringing more news, another report,
That no Jews are left in his sector
But he could truly use some gasoline
Because he supposes and suspects
That the verminous tribe is hiding en masse in bunkers.
The earth will have to be dug and the houses demolished
Or the Jews could be smoked out with fire and flames.
Arson is applauded,
its originator congratulated
And praised by his SS bosses

As this idea is a welcome change from tedious shooting.
Soon flames will surround the buildings
The Jews must die. Such is their destiny.
Old people, women, and children are

Dying in hellish torments. Waves of flame,
As fiery cascades fall
In an avalanche on bunkers and cellars.
Low creeping clouds of smoke,
Now ascend the skies, and overcast the ground.

The sun's golden rays drown in them.
The smoke obscures the daylight.
The air of the ghetto turns gray and gloomy.
The ghetto itself is dying.
All signs of life disappear. From nook to nook,
From cellar to attic, death invades
Its territory, reaps its harvest.
discards the scythe into the trash bin,
As an obsolete symbol fit only for rubbish.
After all, civilization provides modern weapons
Which make the scythe look ridiculous.
Machine guns and various grenades
Provide a better concert when death begins to dance.

LAST SONGS FOR THE DYING

To the beat of the rifles shooting
The last songs are played for the dying
Hand grenades are exploding in the air.
Thus this melody is played,
At times fortissimo and at times andante
This horrible music, this symphony from hell.
Atrocious, savage, and relentless, death is running amok.
Doing its work by the sweat of its brow

In its entire ugliness and horror.
It reaches its finale in this terrible *Aktion*
Conducted under the title of Liquidating The Jews.

AKTION

The *Aktion* once completed,
Is celebrated with a bumper harvest of death.
Jews found their liberation in death.
With great suffering they are burned alive,
Like sinners in Hell,
Summoned into a world of devils,
From the world of shadows,
Tortured,
Martyred.
Expiring in the flames,

A Jewish child showed no fear.
A beautiful girl leaves her hideout to escape
                                the flames
And save her young life.
As soon as she emerges from the hiding place
                                in the cellar
The Prussian police surprise her.
They lead this lovely,
Graceful girl,
To the place of execution.
She refuses to disrobe.
She shows no fear or trembling.
She stands facing her executioners,
With an enchanting smile on her lips.
She will not cower.

She firmly refuses to fear.
She is not frightened of death and curses
                                her executioners.
Yes, she is guilty of being Jewish.
She knows she has to die; such is her fate......
Her face has turned to stone
Making their souls shiver.
Then, one Prussian brute laughs coarsely
                                and orders her to undress.
The girl resists but the Prussian does not shoot her.
Apparently something is restraining him.
The drunken Ukrainians around them laugh wildly
But lack the courage to shoot her too,
And one after another,
They refuse to fire at her.
After a long pause,
A summoned Ukrainian,
Reports that the order has been executed.
After the *Aktion* the Jewish brigade,
Heaps together the corpses of the murdered victims
                                into a pyre
So as to leave no traces of the massacre.
Nothing will be left of them except their memory.
Nothing else, no proof of the slaughter.
Nothing to exhume from the ground even.
The corpses are burned on pyres.
Even the charred bones and mortal remains
Will not be left as mute testimony

Of the bloody deeds of the oppressors.
Pits were dug out
And the remains buried with the ashes blown away.

ATROCIOUS THINGS

Indifferent to their unimaginable torments
The killers decide quickly on lives of thousands
Instantly, without thinking, as long as there are more
They perform their duties willingly, with enthusiasm
All are swept up in the fury of hate
To a side, a barrel of rum stands on the street
It helps when rage threatens loss of reason
Everyone is drunk to the verge of lunacy
Relishing atrocious things
Beating, shooting, and sometimes even hanging people
Deriving great joy from doing so
Their handsome faces shine with enthusiasm
After all, they are famous at home for their toughness
And notorious abroad for their barbarism
Pyres burn in the center of the square
Moans of the wounded, the doomed voices
                              of the burning damned
Rise to the heavens in a hellish glow
Their souls rise in the smoke
All around a thick cloud is forming
A cloud where many live out their last moments

Now and then a henchman comes running...
As if from the field of combat and
Snatches a drink from the barrel
Makes a report, his face that of a hero

Declaring that on his order at this moment
"So many thousands are dying"
While thousands of Jewish Martyrs
Tear the heavens apart with their deaths
He reports in detail
Keeping in mind the plans of the SS
That no blow may be wasted
But dealt with impetus
Weapons rattle in a hurricane of fire
But they are trying to save amunition,
By not shooting unnecessarily
They strike the walls with heads of little children
Which fall off like sunflowers

The Ghetto is burning, the Lwow Ghetto is in flames
Lwow's population is drowning in rivers of blood
Our blood is flowing in rivulets down the gutters
It is gushing from the mouths of its victims
This blood has already covered so much of the earth
Fertilizing tracts of land.

Golden flames of conflageration rise to the heavens
The red fire cuts everything, as if with scissors
It spreads like a flood
Life is sobbing with death
The golden land merges with the heavens
While on the square in the midst of narrow lanes
There continue reports of round-ups carried out
Dozens of luxury cars and young officers
Direct the raid, each personally taking part in it
With a light machine gun or pistol in hand
They all look elegant and handsome

They issue orders, point to victims
Another gorilla wields an iron bar
Reaching the Earth's summit
Atlas tortures poos women
Cracking their skulls

THE WORLD OF DEVILS

With the machine gun trained at us
I try to avoid the fire so as not to get hurt
The soldiers deployed around the fire
Keep firing; to them it is a game
The flames, the illumination
Causing the Jews' liquidation
A big crowd is gathered in the square
The fittest Jews are selected,
To formed a special brigade
To search cellars thoroughly
And form a live shield
To protect the killers, those strong toward the weak
But are too craven to expose themselves
To insure that no Jew has actually
Dared to hide himself there
Responding to shouts, the hidden Jews emerged
To the accompaniment of shooting
After the hidden Jews were discovered,
      the brigade was detained
Digging into the earth
With weapons cocked, the tormentors listened
        to the voices
Of other people hidden in nooks of cellars
The soldiers walk around slowly so as not
        to overlook anyone
They uncover hidden branches of sewage canals
They search holes, hideouts, and lairs.

In the darkness a dull silence hovers
In the darkness you at once lose courage
One must raise one's eyes to see the light,
To detect some secret remnant of light
But one sees only the Prussian god
Who watches alertly
Sometimes a child's crying or cough betrays the hideout
It alone suffices to lose anonymity
In the dark holes sit cursed and condemned beings
All this is very bad for our health
One of the children sickens
And sobs despairingly out of pain
To quench the child's crying
The mother embraced it tightly
Never shall I forget the sound of that wailing
The horrible destruction of a child

      During the *Aktion* the bunkers are emptied
      Their occupants furiously beaten
      Their road to death usually leads
      To a death camp
      Finally, the roundup is ended
      Death has reaped an abundant harvest.
      Every Jewish child
      Found its salvation in immediate death
      Suffering terrible, hellish torment
      Their cries and lamentation rising
      From the world of devils, the world of death.

One condemned man sobbing in front of the flames
Is going naked to his death
On the street roam masses of dirty soldiers
The earth has to be dug, buildings have to be demolished
Smoke and fire have to be used to drive people out
                    of their bunkers…

THE DEATH BRIGADE*

THE DEATH BRIGADE

When ordered to hold hands,
Naked, in fives they enter the other world.
The machine gun clatters
And the executioner finishes his job.

The death brigade places in stacks
Thousands of naked human corpses.
So terrible is the destiny
Of the people that call itself Chosen.

As soon as the bodies burn in the fire,
The Brandmeister** finishes his job.
We condemned men also search for
Trophies with our hands

It is hard to endure the terrifying moans
Of the martyred souls of our brothers,
In ashes we find jaws
Of mouths that can no longer lament.
When Freedom Bell rings,
When the call of revenge is heard
There will be terrible consequences,
The enemy's blood will flow in streams.

---

* The Death Brigade were inmates forced to destroy the evidence of the crimes of the Nazis

** Brandmeister (German for fire chief) was the name used for the Sonderkommando prisoner charged with starting the fire for burning the corpses.

LYCZAKOW FIELDS

When the sky is blood-red
When the stacks of bodies are burning
When the earth is drowning in Jewish blood,
The horrible fate of the Jew is fulfilled.

The wind scatters the smoke rising from the dead,
The wind is blowing from Lyczakow fields,
As death reaps its terrible harvest
With the firing of flesh-ripping dum-dum bullets.

The enemy forces us
To dip our hands in our brothers' blood.
Despite the rage in our hearts
We still laugh and joke.

We are the death brigade
We are the Jewish Holocaust
Engaged in the dance of death
We plan our coming escape.

We hear the moans of our brethren
Who walk boldly into the fire of the flames
We see how the killers torture them
Before sowing death from their guns.

IN THE HIDEOUT
The cellar

LICE

Lice have appeared in our hole under the ground
All at one there appeared three
Three is nothing much, three is a little.
Even a child would not fear them
But very soon there appeared
Not three but six
Six is not three
Six is double
The environment appears good for them.
Then we began to ponder
From whence this assembly of lice came
What road did they take to travel here?
Now that they multiply and are everywhere.
One person is of the opinion
That lice reproduce in a woman's hair
Another is outraged
And claims that lice come from a person
     who does not scratch himself.
The third rediscovers the old tactic
Of using gasoline to kill lice
The fourth wants to kill lice with strychnine,
Something that would kill everybody.

Perhaps he wanted to die himself
Or to attain unconsciousness.

The lice are impervious to this conference
And continue to bite everywhere.

Now that we all keep scratching,
I feel close to Jewish misery,
Now that my wrists are chained,
Now that Devils direct the world,
Plunged into the depths of misfortune,
I believe that in this misery, too, life goes on.
In this cellar, within its confined space,
Live not people, but unfortunate Jews

IN THIS CELLAR

In this cellar
Are crowded
Two dozen shadows
This black inhuman hole
Houses dehumanized Jews, *les miserables.*
The airless, sultry summer night
Keeps us awake
The calm is disturbing
Harbinger of a storm
Now and then the silence is broken
By the sinister clatter of boots.
The music or terror resounds
This is the Prussian war hymn.

The sounds slowly ebb
And silence reigns again.
Everyone avers that this too shall pass.
Something different and more terrible may come.
All over the city on the Prussian wall posters
Goebbels hurls his insults in our faces.

WE KNOW NO RAYS OF THE SUN

We know no rays of the sun,
Our eyes are dulled by gloom,
There is no end to suffering.
The Prussians are choking us.
United by the same misery, are we
Struck by all the same blows of the enemy, are we
Each living shadow
Still loves its own self and voice.
Share the same language
We are the same people,
We know not each other in adversity
And herein lies our moral dilemma..
    This is no sad fairy tale,
      No figment of somber imagination,
      This shapeless mosaic of bodies
      Inside this cellar hole.
We sit in silence,
Tensely, nervously.
On every face the same expression
Of great despair.
Or we play card games,
Not to win but to pass the time
For hours and hours
Awaiting our fate.

MY DEAR

*(A birthday poem for Lusia Sicher, a young inhabitant of the hideout,
probably written by Mrs. Kessler)*

On this your thirteenth birthday,
A special day unlike other days,
Accept my heartfelt wishes
For a happy birthday.
For we love each other
Even if we sometimes spar
Today you have a happy face
Even if you are thought unfortunate.
To me you are always nice
Although sometimes you are mischievous.
Although you are still a child
You already display feminine charm.
I think therefore, my dear
That you will become like me.

May you always remain what you
Are now in our hideout,
May these years be to you
Years of reflection and not of anger.
We are all hiding in the cellar,
Old and young, no matter what age.
When somber fate turns around
And we finally leave this hole,
Accept your age-old suffering
And be a Jewish woman-this is your destiny.

MEMORIES

To this day I remember: On Berka Street,
On the ground floor of a stone tenement,
In a proletarian Jewish apartment,
Among dirty ragged clothing
Lay two inhumanly pale and strange figures
Wearing tattered rags.
Emaciated bodies, wide eyes open,
Vermin everywhere.
The cold shudder passed. I shrugged my shoulders
And exited, moved by that sight of lice-ridden
                                       Jewish misery.

Now it is wartime,
Since then six years have elapsed.
What terrible blows the Prussian whip has dealt us.
Now all the Jews are dying.
Now, I too, live in similar misery.
I hide from the enemy in a cellar.
My body is thin and my eyes are wild,
The cockroaches are all around me.

AT THE EDGE OF HUMAN EXISTENCE

In our cellar hole,
In the blackness of our existence,
We live broken and humiliated,
Awaiting rescue.
Bodies heaped together,
Legs bent,
Pale, chalk-white faces,

Animals, no longer human.
Eyes staring vacantly,
We a lie in a row,
Forced into mutual embrace

Should one of us change his position,
All others,
Turn over to the same side.
Smoke-filled air,
Pervaded by a gray midst,
We breathe hard,
The humid choking air.
At the brink of human existence,
We lead a subterranean life. Because
Without this shelter Death's choking grip awaits us.

OUR HIDEOUT

They walk boldly into machine gun fire.
These visible martyred.
Whom death is stealing away.
Although the enemy ordered us to die
Each of us yearns to survive
Restraining our voices

Although our speech is the same
We do not know each other in the ghetto
Thus is our moral dilemma
Hence our horrible torment
Some unknown somber face
A shapeless mosaic of bodies
Inside this cellar hole
We sit in silence
In this slow cellar torment
On every face the same expression
Of great sadness.

ON OUR SIXTH ANNIVERSARY

Remember? Barely six years have elapsed
Since joined by wedlock we went into the world.
Do you remember the wedding feast, the applause,
Hundreds of good wishes, sent by telephone
                                        and otherwise?
Remember the protracted photographing,
Your gay smile, your posing?
You thought life a whirl of joy,
Bringing us only good.
You believed life was a garden of happiness,
In which the world rejoiced and smiled at you.
My somber gravity always puzzled you,
As did the seriousness of my speech,
And my belief that life demand sacrifices,
That happiness is up to.. [us alone]

Two years of happy memories,
Passed quickly on life's screen
Without any major or tangled problems.
We moved through life in an enchanted dance,
But a horrible moment arrived, the storm of war
Shook the world. In its first assault,
Flooded everything in its raging waves.
Immersing the world in a blood red-rage.

For awhile it separated us.
Courageously, you joined me. You crossed

The green border. How radiant was the moment
　　　　　　　　when we met again.
Across the sand of Sieniawa,* bravely,
　　　　　　　through dark forests and valleys,
You advanced toward me, toward the fulfillment
　　　　　　　　　of your life,
And again we strode together, this time
　　　　　　　　through life's grayness,
Through the stupor of resignation.
　　　　　　　　　How hopeless [we were].
But together once more,
We opened our somnolent eyes
As the reveille of war is sounds again.
As the world sinks in an avalanche
Of fire and iron, and again drowns in blood.
In fetters of brute force man again faints,
When Mars breathes fury. A horrible struggle
For life or death commences, a fight without pardon.
Together again, we stride through
Terrible storms of life, terrible torments,
And we do not know how this struggle will end?
So far, we are neither broken by the storm nor
　　　　　　　　　by the titanic clashes
Of history. We are not broken by the enemies
　　　　　　　　　strength and might.
So then, do not be broken by life's exactions,
By these hellish torments in the cellar hideout.
What can I offer you on this our sixth anniversary?
In the end what can I offer you at all?
May the Lord allow you liberation and release.
I wish you that, your life's fulfillment.

---

* A town near the border between Soviet and German occupation zomes in Poland in 1939.

THE RESCUERS

YOU SURELY REALIZED

You surely realized that we were human beings,
Needing food and help in our laborious struggle.
If we survived by a miracle, that was only because
There are still good people in this world.

You and your child survived this terrible happening
Even though you walked at night braving death,
The child remained alive.

Out of the entire dust of oblivion
Some moments remain unforgettable
Carrying the child you walked to town,
                                          darling Zosienka
To look for bread
Wading through the snow, bending under
                                        the child's weight,
Risking your life
You evaded capture
In the traps set for you.
Yet you survived this hellish adventure together
                                        with the child.
The child's survival is a miracle,
The evidence of your courage.

MEMORABLE SUNDAY

This happened on a memorable Sunday.
Doubting in life, slowly, diffidently,
Driven by despair and fear
We sought shelter under a green roof
                      ...skirting the patrols
Shaken by fear, we crossed the threshold
                      of your home.
You received us cordially and willingly
With your whole heart and soul, your golden soul.
Although the bitterness of life filled our hearts,
You revived us. Our faith in people,
                      and our life instinct returned.
When you told us that we could stay with you,
That you demanded no payment, nothing of us
When you were so hospitable to strangers such as we
I wondered that there could be such people left
                      in this world
So in my life I have met both good and evil
Anxiety that penetrated my body and soul,
                      began to dissipate,
I thought deeply, I wondered about the miracle
                      of our rescue
And I found the answer — you are good people
Today I know that my survival comes
                      only from the miracle
That such brave people are still found on earth.

Four of us unfortunates
Insanely pursued by bloodthirsty enemies
Wondered about your motives

About some justification for your brave deed.
Time passed swiftly. We soon understood your courage.

The raging storm of history
Drove us to your hospitable home
Now I know I owe my survivable to the fact that admirable
people still live in this world.

NOTES

[1] The Germans entered Lwow on June 30, 1941. Before leaving the city, Soviet Security Personnel (NKVD) executed more than 5,000 political prisoners. To Germans and Ukrainians this became a pretext for a program, in accordance with Nazi ideology of blaming Jews for the crimes of the Communists

[2] The unnamed hierch of the Uniate Church, Archchbishop Szeptycki, whom the author mentions elsewhere.

[3] In the USSR the internal passport served as the identity card. The Soviet authorities considered Jews as a national minority.

[4] The city's Reform Rabbi Jecheskiel Lewin, the head of Lwow's Reform synagogue declined accepting the shelter offered him by the Metropolitan and was murdered by the Germans on the same day. Metropolitan Andrzej Szeptycki (1865-1944), the Archbishop of Lwow and head of the Uniate Church, and descendent of a Polish aristocratic family, enjoyed tremendous authority among the Ukrainians of eastern Galicia. In 1941 he greeted German troops as liberators from Soviet slavery. Later, shocked by the brute force applied by the Germans and their Ukrainian allies, he hid Jews in his residence. He also instructed the clergy to save Jewish children. Among others, a son of Rabbi Lewin was saved thanks to his assistance. For more details see: Shimon Redlich, "Sheptyts'kyi and the Jews," in Paul Robert Magocsi, ed., *Morality and Reality: the Life and times of Andrei Sheptyts'kyi* (Edmonton: Canadian Institute of Ukrainian Studies, 1989). Pp. 145 – 164.

[5] This excoriating evaluation of the Lwow Judenrat was fairly common but it should be born in mind that under the German occupation no tactic could protect the Jews against Hitlerite genocide. The first chairman of the Lwow Judenrat, the lawyer Jozef Parnas, an assimilationist, was murdered by the Geramans in October 1941 because he refused to cooperate in the deportation of Jews to an extermination camp. The next chairman, Adolf Rotfeld, a Zionist activist, died in February 1942. The third chairman, Henryk Landsberg,

did not benefit from being submissive to the Germans- he was hanged in September 1942. The last chairman of the Judenrat was Edward Eberson, who was deported with other Judenrat members to an extermination camp in January 1943.

[6] Sholom (Samuel) Schwartzbard (1888-1938), poet and watchmaker, who settled in France in 1920, had witnessed the wave of bloody anti-Jewish pogroms in the Ukraine executed during the 1917-19 civic war in Russia by troops of the Ukrainian People Republic headed by Simon Petlura. On May 25, 1925 Szwarcbard assasinated Petlura in Paris. Ukrainian Nationalists organized a pogrom in honor of Petlura in July 1941 rather than on anniversary of his death.

[7] The ordinance of November 1941 did not establish a ghetto proper but merrily specified the districts in which Jews were authorized to live. A closed ghetto was established only in September 1942, whithin much smaller boundaries.

[8] Bridges was the name applied to railroad viaducts with respect to which a district was named as either before the bridge (pre-bridge) or past the bridge (post-bridge).

[9] *Genickschuss* in German means shot in the neck.

[10] Edmund Kessler interweaves his diary entries with poetry and prose in various parts of the book. Not all of the words are ledgible. The text on pages 71-72 of the original diary are not legible. The poem describes the liquidation of the Lwow Ghetto in June 1943. Jews were hiding in bunkers and some of them actively resisted the Germans who were burning houses and throwing grenades at them.

Part III

SALVATION

As Seen Through The Eyes of Author

Kazimierz Kalwinski

Gliwice, Poland
1998-1999

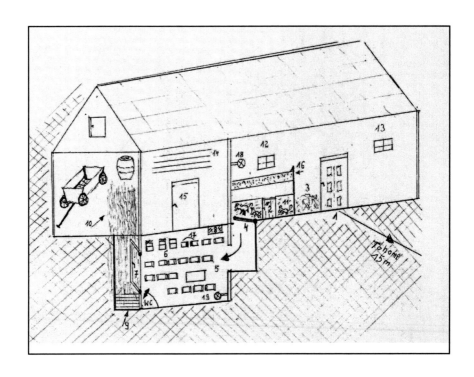

Diagram Kalwinski Bunker.

It was drawn by Kazimierz Kalwinski, approx. 1998

1. Doorway to stable   2. Door to pigs   3. Dung   4. Lapel to bunker   5. Doorway to bunker
6. Bed made of plank   7. Door to bunker   8. Window of bunker   9. Stairs to bunker from outside
10. Branch cover stairs to bunker   11. Pigs   12. Horses   13. Cows   14. Hens   15. Door to hen room
16. Kazimierz`s bed   17. Kessler`s bed   18, 19. Lamps

OUR BUNKER IN LWOW: 1942-1944, WHEREIN 24 JEWISH LIVES WERE SAVED

This memoir was written by Kazimierz Kalwinski, the last living surviving son of Katarzyna and Wojciech Kalwinski.

Preface

The Kalwinski family lived in Lwow, Poland on Warszawska Street, number 167. Our family consisted of six people:

1. Wojciech Kalwinski   1899-1964
2. Katarzyna Kalwinski   1903-1980
3. Jozef Kalwinski   1922-1980
4. Maria Kalwinski   1924-1958
5. Stanislaw Kalwinski   1933-1991
6. Kazimierz Kalwinski   1927-

Our house was located in Lwow's suburbs, 2.5 Km. from the center of the city. For many generations our family had engaged in agriculture and gardening, selling products at nearby market squares. Our biggest crop was cabbage; our largest fruit product was strawberries; and the largest area of our fields was planted with wheat and rye crops. We owned horses, cows, some pigs, and a great many hens and turkeys.

We considered ourselves self-sufficient in food products, which was our redemption during the years 1942-1944. In 1938 we paid our last mortgage debt, and for a short time between 1938-1939 we lived a better life. Then in September 1939 the Germans attacked Poland. I was 12.5

years old and my childhood vanished. Without any transition, I suddenly had to grow up.

No one was willing to work in the fields any longer, and we had to do everything by ourselves. Russia, which occupied Lwow and divided Poland with the Germans, took one third of Poland and the rest was grabbed by Germany.

JEWS IN POLAND

Most of the Jews came to Poland in the 14th century during the reign of King Kazimierz (Wielki), Casimir the Great, who afforded them land and numerous privileges. They came from Spain, Russia, and other countries, fleeing their persecutors. Trade and commerce, as well as various handicrafts constituted their main form of employment. Fewer worked in the fields, or tended animals.

At this time, Poland was a mixture of different nationalities: Poles, Jews, Germans, and other smaller minorities who managed to live together until 1939. In 1939 the population of Lwow hovered at 340,000, comprising 180,000 Poles and 120,000 Jews, the rest numbering Ukrainians and other smaller minorities.

The Jewish community differed from the others. A fairly small number, which graduated from the University in Lwow, became physicians, lawyers, engineers, and academicians. A far larger group became prosperous in trade, but the biggest group of all was comprised of poor Jews looking for work not readily available.

These poor Jews, most susceptible to Communist propaganda emanating from Russia, were misinformed, believing that Russian workers drove in their own cars to work in the factories.

YEARS OF OCCUPATION IN LWOW, 1939-1944

At the end of September 1939, after the pact between Stalin and Hitler, Lwow was occupied by the Russians. On the day they entered

Lwow, I went to the center of the city to deliver milk to a physician, a longstanding customer. I witnessed a horrible sight. On the street were piled a mound of rifles and the Russians were leading Polish soldiers-prisoners into captivity. On the main street I saw a hearse pulled by black horses, on which lay an unusually large coffin draped with a Polish military flag. On both sides of the hearse young Jewish boys repeatedly yelled loudly in Polish, "We are going to bury rotten Poland." These were the poorest who believed the lies spread by Communists promising them a better life. How could they know what would happen to them in two more years? I stood with other people on the sidewalk and screamed something at them (I no longer remember what). Immediately, a young Jew brandishing a gun and a red band (he was no more than 15) came over to me and said, "You don't like something?" Some old man pulled my hand saying, "Go! Go!"

This is how they thanked Poland for accepting their ancestors centuries before. The richer, more intelligent middle class Jews condemned their behavior, but they could do little. Young Communists denounced them and reported them to the Soviets, as they did other Poles, and rich Jews.

The Russians ordered Mr. Sprecher, the owner of the biggest house in Lwow, to leave his house immediately. He climbed to the roof of his house and flung himself to death. The owner of a big farm was also denounced as a "bourgeoisie."

As a result of the denunciations, many Poles and wealthy Jews were exiled to Siberia. Many owners of big farms were also denounced, and our family was prepared for the worst — deportation. Each of us had a sack with necessities ready to go. My father was promptly arrested, when someone reported that he had a colt and a hunting rifle. In fact, he had sold his hunting rifle before the war and no longer hunted. Luckily they believed him and he was released.

Terror reigned in the city because the Ukrainians joined with the Russian Communists in tormenting the Polish population, a situation that continued until June 22, 1942, when the Germans attacked Russia.

Exactly on the 21st day of June, one day before the war, I graduated from elementary school, on the very cusp of another occupation, this time by Hitler.

LWOW UNDER GERMAN OCCUPATION

As I described above, on the day the Germans entered Lwow (at the end of June 1941) I went to our doctor to deliver milk. History repeated itself; local Germans greeted the victorious Nazi soldiers with flowers, giving the Hitler salute.

Having difficulty finding agricultural workers, we were forced to do all the farm work ourselves. My dreams of attending school vanished, because the Germans would not permit middle and Grammar schools to open.

Our family experienced great difficulty, including a bad harvest caused by poor weather in Autumn of 1942 which gave rise to a famine that lasted until the end of summer 1943.

At that time, I had taken a train to the countryside in search of food, exchanging clothing for potatoes, flour, milk, and other foods. Everyday eighteen to twenty people died, mostly poor Jews. The hungry were reduced to eating birds such as sparrows, as well as cats, dogs, and even weeds resembling spinach.

On one of my trips, while boarding a train, I was beaten by a railway policeman, who I learned was doing it for sheer sport.

Barley soup was our mainstay. I consumed the weekly bread ration in one day. For the first time in my life, I walked around constantly hungry. Others were hungry as well. Fortunately, in summer of 1942 our harvest was good. My mother grew vegetables, which I transported by horse to the market (every day) for sale. One day she came home from the market and declared that she would never go there again.

A German woman buying a cabbage from her was enraged that my mother asked her to pay one mark (2 zlotys) for one. She summoned a Gestapo man who twice slapped my mother in the face with thick leather gloves. The woman paid her only half a mark. From this time on, only my sister and I went to the market.

In July of 1942, the Germans forced the Jews into the Ghetto, surrounded it with a wooden fence, which luckily was porous enough for them to buy something in the marketplace. One day when I was throwing cabbages from my wagon, a young boy about five or six years old, approached me and seemed mesmerized by the cabbages. I gave him a big head. Like a little cat, he jumped through the hole in the ghetto fence. He came back a few times, remembering me. I am sure he had no money. Going to the square several times, I helped some Jews take their belongings to the ghetto where they were forced to live. Sometimes I asked for nothing, because I knew they had no money at all.

Once I witnessed a young Jewish policeman leading a group of men to work, beating each with a stick. In the back a German returning from the ghetto followed. I asked him why he beat them, to which he replied, "What did you not like it?" I ran away quickly afraid that he would call a German. I wondered what this war was doing to normal people.

On our street, three homes away from us, lived a Jew named Hoch who had a grocery, an apolitical man liked by everyone. Sometime in July 1942, with part of his family already in the ghetto, his son Sholek came to us with an urgent request: "Kalwinsky save us!" I suggested that we dig out big rocks in the stable where our horses, cows, and pigs lived. We carved out a big opening in the thick wall to make an entrance to the basement with room for pigs. Long branches covered the outside steps to the basement. We nailed together planks to make beds. When the room 5m x 3m was ready people from the ghetto slowly started to arrive. The Hoch family first moved into the bunker which was adequate for eleven people, but as the German liquidated the ghetto, the Jews realized they would have to escape or perish. Little by little, more families arrived. Circumstances became more difficult for them and for us.

Later came the families: Herches, Prokocimer, and the Kesslers*, who came after a short stay with a Polish family. They had to leave when a neighbor and some Ukrainians suspected the family was hiding Jews. Later, Leon Weliczker arrived with a friend. In the end 24 people were in the hiding place. From that time on, it was a struggle of life against death for both the Poles and the Jews.

The Germans, who had started to deport the Jews to camps, began burning corpses of dead and sometimes live or wounded Jews in a valley not far from our house. The smoke was all over the street and made it impossible to eat. This camp was nearby and Leon with his friend Kaczanos both ran away and came to hide with us.

Life inside the bunker required a constant effort from our whole family. All work relating to the proper functioning of the bunker was done by my mother and father, as well as my sister and myself. My brother Jozef married in 1941 and my youngest brother Stanislaw, ten years old in the spring of 1943, was sent to friends in Rzeszow so that at least one member of our family would survive if the Germans discovered the bunker.

Poland had been defeated by the Germans and the threat of death hung over Poles hiding Jews. How does a family who invites 24 Guests for an evening, feel? After they leave, it has their hands full of work. And if they stay for three days, the family needs to provide them with a place to sleep and meals. And what if the come for 670 days? No sense in making comparisons because this was not a visit, but a struggle between life and death for both sides.

---

* Kazimierz Kalwinski gave testimony to Yad Vashem (number 204) in 1982. He mentioned the following people who were hidden in his parents' house: Emmanuel Hoch and his sons, Josko (Ozjasz) and Szulek (Saul) Josko's wife (name not mentioned); Emmanuel's daughter's Bronia Sicher and Munia (Emma); Max Sicher (Bronia's husband); Fryderyk Sicher (Mak's brother); Lusia (Leonora) and Dzidka (Fryda) Sicher, daughters of Maks and Bronia; Maks and Anna Herches with daughter Gaby; Bernard Kuhn, brother of Anna Herches; Edmund Kessler and wife Fryderyka, Mr. And Mrs. Prokocimer, Kaczonos Korman, and Leon Weliczker. The correct spelling of the names was confirmed by the records at the Jewish Historical Institute in Warsaw, Poland.

In this situation there was a division of work for every member of the household. My father and I worked in the fields in order to provide flour, potatoes, and vegetables. Without these, we could not provide enough food for all the people. Mother together with Munia, who hid in our house (the bunker was comprised of 23 persons), and our sister cooked meals and washed clothes late into the night hours. They always had to be in the house because of Munia.

For safety's sake, I always slept in the stable where I had a bed over the pigs. I was in charge of bringing daily water to the bunker and taking out the waste, which I hid in the stable among horses, cows, and pigs.

In the spring I went to the market everyday and sold vegetables. My sister secretly bought the merchandise we needed. My mother brought meals three times a day if there wasn't any danger. My mother carried them in pails. Sometimes meals were once a day, but I will tell about that later.

My mother always prepared meals with the help of Ms. Munia which always took many hours, often late into the night. The windows were carefully covered. Breakfast consisted of coffee made from ground grain with milk from our cow and "zenow" (croissants) baked by Ms. Munia. Lunch usually meant a vegetable soup and a second dish with potatoes and meat (if there was a chance to buy it) or eggs. Supper was similar to lunch.

Our family ate the same meals as the persons in the bunker. Ms. Munia always said that our family didn't have two kitchens. I drank the same coffee that Dr. Prokicimer did. My mother always took the food in towel-covered pails to the stables, always looking around the house to make sure no one was approaching. If someone appeared, we went to the back of the house and hid the pails.

My sister found it hard to get items we needed, such as washing powder and soap, that the farm did not provide. Buying large amounts of merchandise could arouse suspicion. I brought home these goods together with food I obtained for the (Polish) refugees. Since our neighbors knew about it, we could buy large amounts of merchandise for the committee and avoid suspicion.

Another helpful situation was that our yard was surrounded by a big fence separating us from our neighbors. The house was set back 30 meters away from the street. During the time the bunker was in operation I slept above the pigs, with the doors secured by heavy beams, and the windows were covered and dark. Well into the night a light shone which I put out when I went to sleep.

In the evening the men came out of the bunker to the cow shed or the pigstye to use the toilet and walk a bit among the animals. This went on past 1 a.m. Many times I fell asleep earlier, as I worked hard all day from 5 a.m. until 10 p.m. Leon Weliczker (Wells) visited me after work and read his writing about the death brigade which he published after the war. The women, who never went out of the bunker even to take a walk, were in a far worse situation.

From time to time, Szolko went out at night to exchange dollars into zlotys at his friend Rozenkiewiez's house. When his friend asked where he was hiding, Szolko replied that it was better that he did not know. He didn't asked him again. Szolko had a revolver and was ready to use it in case of danger. His leaving the bunker proved to be a nuisance, because he returned very late, and I could only open the door if he uttered a password. I usually did not get enough sleep on those nights, for my work started very early.

At this perilous time, thieves used to break into the stables to steal horses and pigs. One day 10 people were walking in the stable (talk there was forbidden). I heard someone banging at the door. I shouted, "Hey you" and heard the thieves run away.

In the beginning of 1943 Ms. Munia was discovered. She did not have enough time to take cover in the small enclosure when Uncle Karl, my mother's brother, came into the kitchen unexpectedly very early and quietly. He said, "Please don't be afraid." And until the end he never whispered a word about it. But even then, he never knew that there were 24 people hiding there.

When coming home with merchandise, I used to buy the Lwow paper which was then read by everybody. Besides that, people listened to a German radio with a crystal which I bought quietly from a friend, as it was illegal to own a regular radio and we had to give it away (as well as our skis).

There was increasing terror in Lwow. Groups of the AK (*Armia Krajowa* — Polish Home Army) took revenge on occupying soldiers and Ukrainians. Once when I drove the wagon into the square, I saw a drowned Gestapo man in the pond. With my sister by my side, we quickly finished our shopping and went home by a different route. By now, plenty of Gestapo men must surely have gathered there. A Gestapo man, who used to come to a woman on our street after the curfew, slapped young Polish boys on their faces when he saw them on the street. This woman's hair was later shorn to the skull and she walked with her head wrapped in a scarf.

Another time I was stopped by the police for control purposes, who turned everything upside down. I was lucky not to have too much stuff for the bunker and more for the [refugee] committee for help to Poles for whom I carried a bill for storage. When I came home, I found out that our boys from the AK had gone to a restaurant that was reserved just for Germans, for some beer. The Germans became angry and slapped their faces.

Shortly after they left, some of them returned and killed three Germans with machine guns. At the same time, the Ukrainian police went berserk. After the nine o'clock curfew, they stopped the boys asking them for papers. The AK people who went out into the streets after curfew were asked for papers and were immediately shot down.

I recall once coming back from the square when a German driver hit the wheel of my wagon. He was laughed heartily when my horse fell and broke its heel.

In spring 1943, I cut out boards directly above my board bed to let the girls, Lusia, 12, Sudra,* 10, and Gaby, 7, go up to play in the hay. The

---

* The author probably meant Fryda.

overpowering smell of the flowers and hay was so intoxicating that they fell asleep, which gave me a scare. I had to then bring them back down.

I did not go inside the bunker often, because it was far too crowded, but sometimes I sat in the threshold and played cards and related what was happening in town. In the winter of 1943 my brother Jozek and I started to deliver wood from the forest to the German barracks. We had special passes, because we returned late at night. Once traversing in the woods, we found 17 people who escaped from a train and were killed by the Germans. We saw these Nazis and their dogs coming out of the woods. They asked us if we saw any Jews. We told them that we had only seen dead ones. They gave us a scare, but let us go. Until today I remember seeing a young girl about 16, who died holding a piece of bread in her hands.

Sometime in the Autumn of 1943, a funny incident occurred in the evening. One of the pigs chose to sleep in the entrance of the bunker. She also used it as her toilet. Over time, the wood became wet and weakened until one day the wood broke and the pig fell through to the bunker below and emitted a terrible noise. It was quiet and we were afraid someone would hear the noise. We thought we would have to kill her, but with great difficulty we were able to hoist her up. We immediately cut a board and made a new cover which lasted till the end of the war. Thus passed the first year in the bunker.

The Germans began their retreat. Withdrawing from Moscow, Leningrad, and Stalingrad. The people in the bunker rejoiced upon hearing the good news, but suddenly on the sixth of December, 1943, the Germans discovered a hiding place of 34 Jews on Pan Jozefek Place, 1 kilometer from us. Their downfall was a quarrel so loud that it was heard by a Ukrainian policeman passing by. He called the Germans. They took the Jews together with the two sons of Mr. Jozefek and hung them on one of the city squares, leaving them there for three days as an example for people to see. They pinned a card to them "Hiding Jews". They freed the father, who was taking care of a small grandson, because he claimed he did not know anything about it.

I wanted to go see the awful sight, but my father asked me to stay home and I listened to him. The news caused the people in our bunker to break down, declaring they intended to leave, so as not to further endanger the lives of our family. "But where to?" asked my father, "If they get you they will find out about everything anyway." They accepted the logic of his reasoning. All of them prepared poison to use at the last minute. Sholko decided to get additional weapons in case of the bunker's discovery. "Let the Germans pay a price!" He gave me the address of his friend, a Pole, in order to ask him for a revolver and ammunition. One Sunday, I went there and rang the bell. "What do you want?" I heard a woman's unsympathetic voice. I told her I came to see her husband. He came out and politely asked what I wanted. I responded that I was sent by Sholek Hoch. "He is alive!" He exclaimed, jumping for joy. He wanted to know where he was. "It's better if I don't divulge the details," I told him. He took out money but I said I didn't need it. Sholek needed a revolver and ammunition. The man promised he would try to get it in a week, at which time I could come and pick them up. He sent his greeting to Sholek and I left quickly, afraid of his unpleasant wife. I did not go back to get the weapon, because Sholek changed his mind. When they met after Sholek left the bunker, the man was very offended. He went through great danger to get the weapon realizing Sholek's perilous situation.

Life resumed its normal rhythm and so passed the winter of 1943.

The front was moving closer everyday, but the Germans stubbornly defended their positions. In spring of 1944, the Russians started to bomb Lwow. In the beginning the attacks consisted of irregular air raids, but soon they happened everyday after 9 p.m. When they bombed the railway station and airport, the tremors could be felt in the bunker, where great joy pervaded among the hiding Jews.

I was standing with my father in the yard at 9 p.m. when My father said the Russians would not come (he was hard of hearing). I said, "They're coming now!" I'm hearing a threatening noise. An instant later, the bombs fell and the Russians lowered huge lights which lit up the whole city, almost turning it into day.

In April they began to bomb during the day. We thought the end of the war was near, but the hardest days still lay ahead of us. One day toward evening, we were shelling peas and beans, when we heard approaching planes. I looked up and saw bombers and fighters directly above us. I quickly counted bombers and 50 fighters. I had never seen so many planes! They flew over our house and divided into the sky. Some of them bombed an artillery post nearby that did not have a chance to return fire. This marked the beginning of the German retreat. Almost everyday, groups of German soldiers came to our yard, spreading out boards on tables, eating their food and running off.

Once the Germans spread themselves out a mere five meters from the bunker. We had two pigs, which dove under the stairs of our home. Sitting in front of our house, I gave them the best flour and water we had. A soldier approached on a motorcycle, looked around, and then after him a big platoon arrived, which spread itself out to eat food. I heard a tiny squeak. My father asked me if the Germans heard anything. I didn't know, but I knew I had heard it. After half an hour, as if by miracle they all left. We had luck. It was the same everyday, although the troops who left took our horse.

Two weeks before the Russians arrived, their aircrafts started flying overhead and shooting at the German troops. Then the worst thing happened; a platoon of German soldiers and their horses arrived at our house. Some of their horses were put into the stable, but there was no room for the rest. Their commander ordered us to throw away wood which covered the stairs leading to the bunker, because he wanted to put the rest of the horses there under a roof. Some of the soldiers started to remove the branches off, whereupon father showed them that the barn could, in fact, hold more horses. The Germans looked and said that the beam would not allow the additional horses to enter the barn. Father immediately brandished the saw and cut down the beam. The horses were then put into the barn. Slowly, my father put back the branches in their usual place. In a second, an airplane flew overhead, but the pilot didn't see any horses. I didn't witness this because according to plan, I ran to our neighbors who lived 1.5 kilometers from us. I went to their garden and waited for awhile. I knew that if the Germans found our bunker a lot of shooting would ensue because they would kill everyone. Later, I saw my father looking around (the aircraft had by then flown away) and called to me. He then told me what happened. Five more minutes and we all would have been dead. Five minutes made the difference between life and death. Only God protected us.

I went to the room where the Germans had been and saw a German machine gun behind a mirror. I really liked it, but when I showed it to my father, he told me, "Better leave it in place." And again, God was watching over us. In ten minutes a soldier on a motorcycle comes into the room to retrieve his gun. Can you imagine what would have happened if the gun hadn't been there? Indeed, it isn't hard to imagine. That was our last visit from the Germans.

I went out on the street and saw some soldiers around the house. They were Russian soldiers asking about the Germans. Behind them, came more soldiers in cars, many tanks and cannons. It was the end of July 1944 and singing of Russian soldiers filled the air. I came back to the bunker, opened it and said, "It's over!" The soldiers' singing could be heard in the bunker, from which came a loud "Hurrah!" And as was our custom, I cautioned, "not so loud."

AFTER THE LIBERATION

After the liberation, every evening we started to let a few people go. The Hoch family stayed three days longer, because someone else was occupying their house. At first, we helped our occupants with some food, as they had nothing. We had all lost much weight. My mother weighed 44 kg. After the liberation and started to faint from weakness. My sister also started to become ill. My weight was 62 kg. (today I am 98 kg.) and my father was also sickly. So ended our "Gehenna."

Some of our acquaintances suspected that because we saved Jews we made riches. We did not save human lives for money.

After 17 months of occupation by the Russians, we had to leave Lwow, on December 24, 1945, as it was handed to them by England and America. We loaded our two wagons, the first wagon with horses (bought from Russians) and a cow; in the second, our family. We were entering the unknown. We settled in Gliwice, Poland on January 2, 1946.

After the liberation, life was difficult for our family. My father sent me to school and I went on to study in Wroclaw. This incurred further expenses for my family. They sent me a little money, and potatoes and beans. Sometimes I was so hungry that I had to visit old friends from Lwow for dinner. In Wroclaw, I lived in a small room which was given to me by my friend Szolko for free.

During my second year of studies, I quit because I didn't want to be a burden to my parents. I returned to Gliwice and started to work first as a teacher and then as a director of a school. My parents were happy that we were together.

In 1951, my brother Staszek finished grammar school with honors and passed the examination for the Polythechnic Academy. He didn't go there in the end because he got work in an orchestra and started to work freelance as a musician. He settled in Cracow where he had his own jazz band called, "Drazek and Five" *(Drazek I Piecu)*. Drazek (stick) was his pseudyonym. He also studied mathematics which he finished five years later.

My father became ill and his condition worsened. I employed my mother, because it was necessary for her to work in her old age. Occupants of our bunker went all over the world and some stayed in Poland. During the holidays (twice a year) they sent us gifts from abroad. We sometimes got oranges and clothes, but this did not solve our everyday financial hardships.

In 1953 I married my wife and we lived with my parents. My son Stazek was born in 1955, and in 1960 my daughter Ewa. It was hard times and my wife couldn't work. In 1958 my sister died. She was only 34. She paid a high price for the war and our bunker. In 1963 my brother Staszek went on scholarship to the Boston School of Jazz. When he finished in 1964, my father died. Staszek started to work for IBM (as there was a great deal of competition in music). He sent money regularly to my mother. My mother started to work as a gardener in an orphanage where my wife worked. After she broke her arm, she retired and cooked dinner for us everyday. She died in 1980 when she was 77, sixteen years after my father, who died when he was 65. In 1980 my brother Jozef also died, he was 58. My parents went through the hardest of times from 1946 to 1965. Poets say that you can't transplant old trees. For us children, it was much easier to find work. For them (especially my father), it proved to be much, much harder. Despite many gifts from the occupants of our bunker, my parents still struggled.

In 1984 I was honored by Yad Vashem, as were my late my parents. A tree is planted in their honor. I planted a tree in Jerusalem "Zasluzony Wsrod Narodow Swiata" (Righteous Among the Nations) and also received a medal. I became "Honorary Citizen of Karmiel" where Lusia Sicher lives in Israel. Prior to that, Edmund Kessler visited us in Gliwice. We fed him 'pierogi' (a traditional Polish dish; boiled dough pockets filled with meat, cheese, or fruit) which was Mr. Kessler's favorite.

I managed to finish the Faculty of Technology at the university. The last five years of my career, I worked as inspector of schools. I retired in 1982, after a heart attack. In 1968, my brother Staszek visited us in Poland after 23 years. He died five years later in 1991, and his remains stayed with our mother in Gliwice.

I am now retired, working in the garden as much as my health permits and my legs can take. All that is left is the memories of those horrible year of Hitler's occupation and the people with whom we survived together. Often, I ask myself the question: "What would I do now if, God forbid, if the same situation repeated itself?" I answer that as in the years, 1942-1944, I would do the same thing. Because a human life is worth as much as we can help other people.

This short story about the years 1942-44, I dedicate to the daughter of the Kesslers, Ms. Renata Kessler, in memory of the ordeal which her parents and I lived through.

I extend my thanks to my grandson Maciej Matecki for his assistance with the manuscript. Written 1998-1999, Gliwice, Poland.

Marker for Wojeich and Katarzyna Kalwinska at Yad Vashem

Stone rubbing of list of survivors from Yad Vashem

Jerusalem 1984

Yad Vashem

"Words of deepest gratitude
Put together for unforgotten sons and daughters [of Poland]
Wojciech and Katarzyna Kalwinski
Noble and big Poles
People of rare bravery and goodnes
Who exposed their family and their lives to great danger
Saving 24 Jews during the blodthirsty German occupation
Of Lwow during the years 1942–1944
Here is a stone rubbing of those who were saved: 1–24."

Kazimierz Kalwinski

LUSIA'S LETTER

Lusia Sicher

January, 2, 2004

Dear Renata,

Forgive me for delaying with your request to write about my experiences for so long. Still, after all, writing about them is in my own interest, as it matters to me that the name of my uncle, who organized it all, be mentioned in the book. In our country (Israel), life is always tense, so it is difficult to find the patience to write.

I shall try to write down what I remember about my two year stay in the bunker. Mr. and Mrs. Kalwinski were like angels; they were aware of the penalty for sheltering Jews, yet they took the risk and agreed to give us refuge. They used to be neighbors of my grandfather.

There were 24 of us in the bunker, with nearly one-half being my family members. My mother's brother Saul Hoch organized it all, and we owe our survival to him too. Your parents were with us. My uncle brought them from another home. My mother along with her sister and the Prokocimer couple, husband and wife, had been sheltered there.

I liked your father very much. He was a wonderful man, calm and very patient. He liked children and was the only one in the bunker to play with us. At the time, I was eleven, my sister was five, and there was one more little girl Dziunia, older than my sister but younger than I.

I find it hardly conceivable nowadays how 24 people could spend two years doing nothing in a cellar. The hygienic conditions were very bad, yet no one fell ill. In the daytime a small bulb glowed, but it had to be extinguished in the evening as its light, shining through a crack in the tiny window, might attract somebody and betray us. The window onto the street was blocked with a bench. The entrance to the cellar was through a hole in a pigsty; the hole was covered with boards and straw, and the pigs lay on it. One time the boards rotted and collapsed so that a pig, squealing, dropped on us. I recall how it was hoisted back up with ropes.

To enter the cellar, all the obstacles had to be moved aside before sliding down into the hole. Climbing out of the hole was more difficult; the men somehow made it on their own, but the women and children had to be hoisted. In the evenings we left the cellar one by one to satisfy our physiological needs, covering the results with cow manure.

Mr. Kalwinski agreed to hide us, but his son Kazimierz (Kazio) and daughter Maryla did most of the hard work. They shopped for food for so many people. At the time, Mr. Kazimierz was a teenager and had such big responsibilities. He slept on a cot, in the loft above the pigs and watched out at night so that neighbors would not discover us. The shed contained not only pigs but horses, cows, and goats. My mother's sister Emma Hoch cooked for us all but did not stay with us. She stayed in a kitchen shed outside the house. In that shed she did the cooking and worked very hard. If not for her, we could not have stayed there and survived.

The cellar door was covered with boards and on top of the boards were straw and bedding. We slept side by side. I remember how at night everyone turned over at the same time because space was so tight. One corner was turned off, and behind the curtain was a washing bowl on a stand and two pails, one with clean water and the other for dirty water. I don't remember how long the allotted time intervals for washing were.

Shortly before our liberation, biting insects (lice) appeared and had to be hunted down to keep from multiplying.

Kazio provided us with water in a pail and had to pull up the pail with dirty water. In addition, we had to do laundry.

My uncle, mother's brother, Saul Hoch, risked his life on occasion, by leaving the cellar at night (to go down to Lwow — we lived in a suburb) to see a friend in order to exchange dollars or to sell jewelry for our survival. We always felt worried until uncle came back.

Mrs. Kalwinska brought us food daily in three pails. There was a bench in the cellar with space for three people and we sat on it in shifts to straighten out our backs. In the evenings we climbed out in pairs, female and male alternately to relieve ourselves.

There was not enough air in the cellar and we children often were raised to the level of the window in order to breathe fresh air. The window itself was blocked with a small bench, which made it impossible to look inside. The children and young men stayed longer in the shed above, which also served as a stable for horses. We could pat the horses and sometimes we were raised and let to sit on a horse for a little enjoyment.

One evening Mr. Kazimierz took us up to the loft above the stable, which was lined with freshly mowed hay that smelled so good. We were finally allowed to enjoy the sight of the moon and the starry firmament.

Just before the liberation something serious happened, that almost ended in tragedy. One rainy day, Germans retreating from Lwow arrived on horseback and stopped at the Kalwinski house. They demanded the removal of the boards covering up the entrance to our cellar. They wanted to leave their horses there because the place had a roof, thus protecting the horses from the rain.

We listened to their shouts and thought that was the end of us. We were prepared for the worst. Among us were the Prokocimers, a married couple, who kept poison (cyanide pills) for such an eventuality. Mr. Kalwinski ordered his son to leave the house, so as to stay safe.

Mr. Kawinski saved his family and us by his cleverness. He brought out some vodka to the Germans and offered them his barn, which solved the problem. He saved his family and twenty-four people from death.

Mr. Kalwinski used to visit us once a week. He found it difficult to slide down the hole into the cellar and even more difficult to climb back up. He was very corpulent. He used to bring us news of the world and give us encouragement and hope that the war would soon end.

One time they brought us very sad news. Several houses away thirty-five Jews were discovered and two brother, members of the Jozefek family, who had given them shelter, were hung in the center of Lwow. They were left hanging for a week to demonstrate the fate awaiting people who wanted to save Jews. My uncle told Mr. Kalwinski that we would leave that very night and everyone would save himself the best that he could. Mr. Kalwinski said that since he had sheltered us so long, he would continue to shelter us until the liberation. He was a great hearted man!

Greetings,

Lusia and husband.

P. S. I wish you a healthy, safe, and prosperous New Year 2004.*

---

* In August of 2004, Edmund Kessler's daughter went to Lviv — the former Lwow — to search for the bunker. She was accompanied by her cousin, Anna Kessler Fiertag. Renata writes about her experiences in the epilogue, *The Search*.

Part IV

EPILOGUE

THE SEARCH

Renata Kessler

Written In Memoriam — May 31ˢᵗ, 2005, U.S.A

It was Father's Day, nine years after my father's death in 1985. It had taken me almost a decade to return to his grave.

My mother had said she wasn't up to it, so I came by myself. As I drove up to the cemetery at Sharon Gardens, in New York, a distinct thought came vividly, suddenly to mind, in my father's unmistakable voice: *So, you finally came.* It was as if he had been waiting for me all that time. In the months and years which followed, I would periodically return to the grave and ask for guidance, especially before important events. On one occasion, another thought came distinctly to mind: *You don't know what you can do until you try. Write a book about history.*

I thought "history" meant "art history," since art had been the central focus of my life since childhood. Time passed, however, and the idea faded.

Several years later, my mother passed away. It was from the papers, letters, and journals that I inherited upon her death that a story emerged. It became clear to me that it wasn't art history to which my father's voice had alluded, but our own family's history.

I knew instinctively that some important cataclysmic event had taken place. I couldn't remember it, but knew it had altered my life forever, and stood ominously between me and the world. In ways I couldn't explain, I couldn't give my entire presence to life. A part of me that I couldn't reach was missing, and no one could fix it.

I gradually came to realize that it was my denial of the Holocaust and its trauma.

* * *

I was born in 1946, virtually on the funeral pyre of my family and my people. I always knew I was different from other children, as if I'd been born wearing an invisible H, for Holocaust, like a scarlet letter. Other children seemed to avoid me; I was different. I wondered if I bore a faint scent of the death camps which my parents had narrowly escaped.

My parents had been living in a refugee camp in Vienna at the time of my birth. Mentally and physically exhausted, and having nowhere to shelter me, they wanted to put me up for adoption. A young nurse, who later became a nun, said to my mother, "Don't give her up. She is so beautiful! I will help you." And Schwester Hilda became my first nanny.

When we moved to America she sent me her wedding picture. She was beautiful, dressed in a white gown with flowers in her hair. "Where is her husband?" I asked my mother. "I think she married Jesus," said my mother, much to my bewilderment.

Before the outbreak of World War Two, my father had been a lawyer in the Polish city of Lwow (now known as Lviv, in the Ukraine.) A few years after the war, we left Vienna, where my father had been Chairman for the International Committee for Jewish Refugees and Concentration Camp Internees, and resettled in America. My father said that he did not want to raise me among [former] Nazis.

Growing up in America in the 1950s, I wanted to be like other children. I wished my family were like the ones I saw on television serials such as "Father Knows Best" and "Ozzie and Harriet." I felt I had missed the mark and was disappointed with my parents for not fitting in. I was too young to understand what they had been through.

It is only in my adult years that I am coming to understand the significance of my past and how it has shaped me. It is this hidden past that has led me on a search for my identity.

The search began in 1994, during a trip to Europe, but had really started eleven years before, while pursuing my Master's degree in art. Themes of ancient, lost and destroyed civilizations began to surface in my paintings, and one of the other students in my class asked if I was the child of survivors. I asked her how she knew.

"It's a recurring theme in your artwork," she said. "We children of survivors have a special radar with each other. You ought to look into it more deeply." She suggested a therapist in the field, Yael Danieli. I called her, but never followed up. I wasn't ready.

After my mother's death in 1996, I began to translate my parents' letters and papers and came upon my father's journal/diary, written primarily in Polish, about his observations and experiences during the Nazi reign of terror. It was the story of my parents' survival and the Christian farmer and his family who had hidden them, along with 22 other Jews, in an underground bunker.

I wrote a letter to the farmer's son, Kazik — a central figure in my parents' survival — to notify him of my mother's death, and to ask if he could tell me about the bunker. A series of letters went back and forth, and he invited me to Poland to come meet him. It was as if he had the key that opened the door to the past.

Our meeting was a happy occasion. I felt as if we had always known each other. The love and gratitude I felt for him and his family were beyond expression. It was then that we conceived the idea of writing a book about history, our history, for this is not only a story about Jewish persecution and the destruction of a people. It is also the story of Christians who risked their lives to save Jews.

After visiting Auschwitz, I realized what a narrow escape my parents had had. One chance in a million had become my chance to live, and as fate would have it, the telling of this story has become my responsibility. It is a continuing adventure that has taken me to Israel and Poland several times. I began to communicate with my cousin Ilana, in Israel, whom I had known only from pictures and stories. Her father was my mother's older brother. He had studied medicine in Italy before the War, and later escaped to the Middle East. Later, he became a prominent psychiatrist in Israel.

This was during a time of intifada in Israel, and I wasn't sure if it was safe to visit. It took me another year to get there — only after Ilana came to the to visit me in the U.S. in 1999 and offered to take me back with her. As it turned out, I left a week after her departure and arrived at Ben Gurion Airport by myself. After some confusion at the airport and the help of friendly strangers, Ilana found me and took me home with her to Herzlya.

It was a unique experience to be in the Jewish state. It had been my father's dream as a young Jewish Nationalist. However, his mother, and later his wife, prevented him from going. My mother believed there would never be peace there, and she was tired of war.

In some ways Israel was like America, a tapestry of people from different cultures, races, and nationalities. In the Jewish State, most of these people of different races were Jews, brought together after thousands of years of exile in the Diaspora, and returning now to their ancestral home.

Guess what Ma? I wanted to tell my mother. *Here it's okay to be Jewish.*

"That's the whole idea of this place," said Ilana, when I told her of my imaginary conversation. Ilana and I exchanged the fragmented stories we had both inherited of our families from pre-war Poland, and she seemed to know even less that I. She was a strong *sabra*, accustomed to a rugged life. "There was nothing here when my parents came," she told me. "We Jews made the desert bloom! We built everything from nothing with our bare hands."

I had only been at Ilana's house for a short time when Sarah called, from Jerusalem. When I heard her voice, years of separation disappeared. Sarah, a writer and journalist in Jerusalem, had been a close friend during my youthful college days. She was so excited that I had come. She acted as if I was her special guest, and without fully knowing it, perhaps I had come to see her again. I told her I had come to find my Jewish identity, and she took it upon herself to help me. We went to a seminar for Orthodox women on the first night of my arrival in Jerusalem. I did not fully find my Jewish identity that night, but I did rediscover our friendship.

Almost 30 years had passed; the body had grown older, but the soul was still effervescent. The spirit of joy and discovery was still as it had been when we were young. Nothing had changed, yet everything had changed. Sarah was married with six children, and lived an Orthodox life in Jerusalem. I was a teacher in America, an individualist who borrowed whatever I felt I needed from a variety of cultures and religions. But something of myself was missing, and whatever it was, I was instinctually seeking it in Jerusalem.

Sarah was the first bridge I crossed, bringing me closer to my true self. Even though we were living different lives, in different parts of the world, my search had brought us together. We talked most of the first night away. The fact that 30 years had passed had little meaning. We were in a time warp and it took several days for us to move into the present.

When Sarah had first moved to Israel many years ago, she had told me, "My soul is in a golden place." Those words stayed with me over the years. Now at last I understood their meaning. The spiritual energy of Jerusalem was high. It was an important place for Jews, Christians and Moslems. I went to the Kotel with Sarah, the Western Wall, known as the "Wailing Wall" to the Jews, the remnant of the destroyed Second Temple. Jews from all over the world come there to pray. Thousands of years of prayers manifested a high energy that permeates the city.

We prayed together at the Kotel. I had a long shopping list for God, but felt as if I was being given the wisdom to ask only for God's blessings, leaving the specifics to divine intelligence. It was Sarah who inspired me to write about my quest for my past and call it *The Search*.

* * *

My search took me to Karmiel, where I found Lusia, who had been a little girl when she was hidden in the bunker with her family and my parents. As I entered Karmiel, I read the signs that said "Welcome to Karmiel, from Holocaust to Resurrection." My eyes filled with tears. I could feel proud of being a Jew here. I did not have to hide or cover up. I told Lusia my idea for the book and later, she sent me her own memoirs in a letter. Another survivor of the bunker whom I encountered, Leon Wells, would ultimately write the foreword to this volume.

On Tisha B'Av, I visited Yad Vashem and took a picture of the marker and tree planted to honor the farmer and his family who had saved us. I found it after much searching. The site was covered with piles of stones, placed there as a sign of respect by the survivors of the bunker and by their children and grandchildren who had come to honor them. In the Jewish tradition, one lays stones to honor the lives of loved ones no longer here. I paid my respects to my relatives who had perished in the camps and ghettos, and to those who had saved us.

There and then, I felt that the farmer and his wife would have wanted me to publish my father's diary in Polish as well as English, so that the Polish people would know that amidst the most horrific circumstances, ordinary people did noble things. My existence is testament to it.

I hardly slept my last night in Jerusalem, overwhelmed by my emotions. I was anticipating my trip to Poland. It was still dark when Sarah and I left Jerusalem in a rental car, headed for Ben Gurion airport. I was on my way to visit my relatives and the son of the farmer who had saved us. I carried pages from my father's diary and a sweater from Lusia for Kazik.

RETURNING TO POLAND

In Israel I found the strength to be Jewish, but returning to Poland I was full of tears; tears of being rejected and severed, and tears of love and gratitude for the Polish family to whom I owe my life. I returned to Mother Poland *to find my identity and make my peace. I returned to find the life that was stolen from me before I was born.*

It was nearly sixty years after the Holocaust when I visited Rzeszow, the ancestral city of my mother. I was 57 years old. The old part of Rzeszow, where my mother lived with her family, was enchanting, with its cobblestone streets and antique houses that dated back centuries. I was amazed to actually be there: a place that had only existed in my mind was now a dream come true. It was difficult to believe that this fairy tale city had turned into a horrific nightmare, for my family and the other Jews of Reisha, *most of whom perished in the crematoriums of Auschwitz and Belzec.*

Walking down the quaint cobblestoned streets of *"Reisha,"* (the affectionate name given it by its Jews) I longed to recapture the life I might have had, but was powerless to undo the history that had robbed me of my extended family's love — the family I might have had — just as I had been powerless to revive the part of my parents that was crushed by the war.

Many Jews were savagely murdered by those who wanted their property and hated their existence. It is unfortunate that even after the savage massacre, the lessons of the Holocaust have still not been fully learned. People still hate Jews and the existence of the Jewish state.

LWOW/LVIV

I had waited all my life to come to Lwow, "the City of Lions," the city of my father's ancestors. Returning to this place where Jewish life was almost destroyed was difficult, but I was reassured by a voice on the phone: "I think what you are doing is very important. We will meet you at the airport."

"What do you call your group?" I asked.

"The Jewish Revival of Galicia."

I was to become part of this revival, just by going back and retracing the steps of my past. The Jewish community of Lviv assisted me by providing me with a guide, an interpreter, and a driver. The Lviv of today is considered the most European city in the Ukraine. Its architecture equals Krakow, Paris, and Vienna. It was meaningful to me that I was here with my cousin Anna, from London, because our fathers played here together when they were children and remained close throughout their lives. Their roots had been in the "Old City." It became obvious to me that the Kesslers were an intelligent and dignified people; a large family of substance and accomplishment in law and in business. The houses reflected it, as did their liquor factory and associated businesses.

During the Second World War, my father had remained in Lwow and was forced into the Ghetto. He performed hard labor in the Janowska Concentration Camp. He was fortunate to have escaped with his life and — like Anne Frank — blessed to have been hidden with my mother in an attic with several other Jews. Due to suspicions by the neighbors, my parents had to leave, which was when a Polish farmer came to their rescue. He led my parents and the other Jews to safety in the farmhouse on the outskirts of Lwow, where my parents spent a total of almost two years until the liberation.

Lviv with all its beautiful architecture was very impressive, but seeing the simple farmhouse where my parents were saved was the most significant part of my journey. My life emanated from this place. I think of it as "the house of my salvation." It glows in my mind.

Kazik had prepared me well for this trip by writing a short letter of introduction, in Ukrainian, to the family that now lives there. The letter explained that from 1942 to 1944, my family had been saved from the Nazis at this address by Kazik and his family.

I approached the kitchen window and presented my letter of introduction. In Polish, I asked them if I could see the interior of the house. Apprehensive at first, the mother and daughter invited me in. They instinctively knew the importance of this visit, and the history of the house joined us together. With the help of an interpreter, I told them what had happened there — a true life drama about the struggle to survive, experienced by 24 Jews and by the Polish farmer who at his own family's great risk during the bloodthirsty German occupation, had hidden, protected, and fed them for almost two years.

To make the experience more vivid, the poem that my father wrote to my mother on their sixth wedding anniversary, spent in the bunker, was read to the family who now occupied the house. My mother had been about the same age as the young woman who lives there now. As she heard the poem, tears came to her eyes. I, too, felt a chill go up and down my spine. You could almost feel the presence of my parents and those who had been hidden there.

The young woman invited us to come back that evening when her father returned from work. When we returned, he had cleaned away the debris that blocked the entrance to the bunker. With a lamp, he guided us through the small passage and showed us what he thought was left of the hiding place. A large brick wall had been erected in the basement to support the addition of the house. Only a narrow passageway remained, with a stairway that led to where the kitchen had once been. I had heard many stories about the house and the bunker from my parents and from Kazik. Until now it only existed in my imagination, and now I was really inside it.*

I explained to the Ukrainian family that they were very lucky to live in a house where such good things had happened, and I could see that they were very happy to be part of that history by living there. They posed with me for a photograph. It pleased me that the house was inhabited by such a kind family; perhaps not so unlike the family that had saved us.

I have come full circle by connecting to the places and people who are part of the past. Those who were there and those who are descendants may now join together to tell this story. A new generation wants to learn about the Jews of Poland. This book is dedicated to them.

Edited by Sarah Shapiro

---

* After reading *Przezyc Holokaust We Lwowie*, Kazimierz Kalwinski informed me that the bunker was actually in the basement of the Kalwinski economic building where animals were housed, and not in the main house, as the current Ukrainian owner of the house had thought. The bunker was actually 15 meters from the main house where the kitchen was.

AFTERWORD

Sarah Shapiro

Jerusalem, Israel, 2006

As one who has read many personal accounts from the Holocaust, I find myself stunned by the particular power of Edmund Kessler's testimony. In the juxtaposition of his understated, documentary-style recording of events with the raw artistry of his poems, a man and his era come chillingly to life. His voice travels across the widening chasm of years, granting us a glimpse of an unimaginable reality.

Dr. Edmund Kessler, a Jewish attorney in Lwow, was determined to accurately preserve some fragment of his brethren's experience for posterity, even as their world was being utterly destroyed. Our responsibility is not only to him and to Fryderyka Kessler, who as newlyweds lived for two years hidden in an underground bunker with twenty-two other Jews. Nor is it only to the Polish farmer who saved them, in spite of supreme risk to himself and his family.

Our responsibility, above all, is to ourselves. We cannot betray our own history by allowing it to be forgotten.

In the eloquence, integrity and dignity of Edmund Kessler, we find ourselves uplifted by the nobility of an individual's effort to transcend the nightmare that was engulfing him. I am grateful to his daughter, Renata Kessler, whose labor of love made it possible for us too, to bear witness.

Part V

BIOGRAPHICAL STATEMENTS

Dr. Eugene Bergman escaped from the Warsaw Ghetto in 1942 with the help of his family and afterward, until the war's end, survived by pretending to be an "Aryan." After the war he earned a Ph.D. in English at George Washington University and subsequently taught English at Gallaudet University until his retirement. He has co-authored the anthology *Angels and Outcasts*, the play *Tales From a Clubroom*, and the biography *Lessons in Laughter*, all published by Gallaudet University Press. Dr. Bergman has translated the manuscript from Polish into English.

Rev. David Bossman is a Professor in the Department of Jewish-Christian Studies at Seton Hall University in South Orange, New Jersey. He serves as Editor of *Biblical Theology Bulletin*. He received his Ph.D. from St. Louis University, writing his dissertation on comparative midrash in 1973. He then did research at the Ecumenical Institute for Advanced Theological Study in Jerusalem, and took courses at the Hebrew University. Thereafter he taught at Siena College in Albany, New York, and served as Dean of Graduate Studies at St. Bonaventure University in Olean, New York, before coming to Seton Hall University as University Provost in 1985. He wrote *"Nostra Aetate in Cultural*

Perspective" as well as the foreword to John Oesterreicher's book *The New Encounter Between Christians and Jews* (1986). He authored a number of monographs and articles on Jewish-Christian studies. He is Executive Director of the Sister Rose Thering Endowment for Jewish-Christian Studies. Dr. Bossman has written the preface for the *Wartime Diary of Edmund Kessler*

Kazimierz Kalwinski, the son of Wojeich and Katarzyna Kalwinski, was instrumental in the survival of 24 Jews hidden in an underground bunker on his family's farm in Lwow, Poland, 1942-1944. He completed University, Faculty of Technology, after the liberation. He worked first as a teacher and then as Inspector of Schools.

In 1984 he was honored at Yad Vashem, as were his parents. A tree was planted in their honor as "Righteous People Among Nations." He was also given a medal and became "Honorary Citizen of Karmiel, Israel." Kazimierz has written about his wartime experiences for the book.

Dr. Edmund Kessler, a Jewish attorney in Lwow wrote an eye-witness account about the persecution of the Jews in the Lwow Ghetto and the Janowska Concentration Camp between 1942-1944. He also recorded his experiences while hiding in the Kalwinski bunker on the outskirts of the city. After the war, he repatriated to Poland and later was forced to flee from post-war pogroms in Rzeszow and Krakow. Fleeing to Vienna, Austria, he served as Chairman of the International Committee for Jewish Refugees and Concentration Camp Internees from 1946 until 1952. This Committee administered the refugee camps in Vienna including Camp Rothschild through which were processed over 200,000 Jewish refugees. Dr. Kessler was held in high regard by the American Joint Distribution Committee, the U.S. High Commission, the Austrian Government and the IRO.

Dr. Kessler attended the Jan Kazimierz School of Law in Lwow, Poland. He graduated with an Advanced Degree in law in 1931. He was registered with the Bar Association in Krakow and Lwow, Poland.

After emigrating to America, he completed a Master's Degree in Business Administration from New York University in 1958. He worked as an accountant for the New York City Rent and Rehabilitation Commission until his retirement. Mr. Kessler began translating the diary himself shortly before his death. However, he was not able to finish the task which became his daughter's legacy.

Renata Renee Kessler, daughter of Edmund Kessler, teaches English As a Second Language in New Jersey. She is responsible for coordinating the research, transcription, and translation of the manuscript from Polish into English. She has traveled to several continents in pursuit of the story over a ten year period. Ms. Kessler has written about her search for the story in the epilogue of *The Wartime Diary of Edmund Kessler*. Ms. Kessler has traveled to Lviv, Ukraine (formerly Lwow, Poland), Poland, and Israel to research the story. She has prepared the manuscript for publication through the Department of Jewish-Christian Studies at Seton Hall University.

Przemyslaw Murckiewicz graduated from the Theology Department of the Catholic University in Lublin, Poland. In his dissertation he used testimonies gathered from the Yad Vashem Archive. In 1992-1997, he was involved in the Society for Polish-Israeli Friendship. He presently teaches at a Catholic school in Brooklyn and is pursuing additional graduate study in the Jewish-Christian Studies Department at Seton Hall University. Mr. Murczkiewicz contributed to the transcription of the original manuscript.

Dr. Antony Polonsky studied history and political science at the University of the Witwatersrand in South Africa. He traveled to England on a Rhodes Scholarship in 1961 and read modern history at Worcester College and St. Antony's College. In 1970, he was appointed lecturer in International History at the London School of Economics and Political Science. In 1989 he was awarded the title of full Professor.

In 1993 Antony Polonsky was granted the Walter Stern Hilborn Chair in Judaic and Social Studies and was Chair of the Department of Near Eastern and Judaic Studies from 1995 to 1998. In 1999, he was appointed Albert Abramson Professor of Holocaust Studies, an appointment held jointly at the United States Holocaust Museum and Brandeis University. He has also been visiting professor at the University of Warsaw, the Institute for the Human Sciences in Vienna and visiting fellow at the Oxford Centre for Hebrew and Jewish Studies.

Among his numerous publications are "Politics in Independent Poland" (Oxford, 1972); " The Little Dictators: A Gustiry of Eastern Europe since 1918" (Routledge, 1975, Japanese edition, 1993) and "The Great Powers and the Polish Question 1941-1945" (LSE, 1976). He is the editor of numerous books and of "Polin: Studies in Polish Jewry" of which twenty volumes have been published. "POLIN" was the winner of the 1999 National Jewish Book Award in Eastern European Studies and runner up in 2006. He edited Abraham Lewin's " A Cup of Tears: A Diary of the Warsaw Ghetto" (Blackwell, 1988) and most recently "My Brother's Keeper? Recent Polish Debates about the Holocaust." (Routledge, 1990). With Joanna Michlic, "The Neighbors Respond: The controversy over the Jedwabne Massacre in Poland" (Princeton University Press, 2004).

Dr. Polonsky was a founder and is now vice-president of the Institute for Polish-Jewish Studies in Oxford and of the American Association for Polish-Jewish Studies, Cambridge MA. In 1999, he was awarded the Knight's Cross of the Order of Merit of the Republic of Poland

and in 2006, he received the Rafael Scharf award for outstanding achievement in preserving and making known the heritage of Polish Jewry. In 2007 he was awarded the biannual Gantz-Zahler Prize in Nonfiction Publishing by the Foundation of Jewish Culture.

Sarah Shapiro is the author of *Growing With My Children: A Jewish Mother's Diary, Wish I Were Here: Finding My Way In The Promised Land* and other books. She is the editor most recently, of *All Of Our Lives: An Anthology Of Contemporary Jewish Writing.*

Lusia Sicher has written her testimony for Yad Vashem. She now lives in Israel with her husband and family.

Leon Weliczker Wells hid in the Kalwinski bunker with the Kesslers. He participated as a witness in the Nuremberg and Eichman trials. His recollection of his experiences *The Janowska Road* was published by Macmillan and the New York Holocaust Library. Mr. Wells wrote the foreword for the manuscript.

BIBLIOGRAPHY

Bergman, Eugene, *Survival Artist, A Memoir of the Holocaust.* Jefferson, North Carolina, 2009.

Epstein, Helen. *Children of the Holocaust: Conversations With Sons and Daughters of Survivors.* New York: G.P. Putnam's Sons, 1979.

Fogelman, Eva. *Conscience & Courage: Rescuers of Jews During The Holocaust.* New York: Anchor Books, Doubleday, 1994.

Gross, Jan T., *Fear: AntiSemitism in Poland After Auschwitz.* New York: Random House, 2006

Gut, Opdyke, Irene and Armstong, Jennifer. *In My Hands: Memoirs of a Holocaust Rescuer.* New York: A. Knopf Inc. and Random House, 1999.

Kahane, David, *Lvov Ghetto Diary.* Amherst, University Press, 1990.

Kessler, Edmund, *Przezyc Holokaust We Lwowie (Surviving The War in Lwow),* Warsaw: Jewish Historical Institute, 2007

Kessler, Renata, *Seminar For The Wartime Diary Of Edmund Kessler,* Jewish Historical Quarterly, Vol. 4/2008, Jewish Historical Institute.

Marshall, Robert. *In The Sewers of Lvov.* New York: Charles Scribner's Sons, 1990.

Paldeil, Mordecai. *The Righteous Amond The nations: Rescuers of Jews During The Holocaust.* Jerusalem, Israel: Jerusalem Publishing House and Random House, 1999.

Richman, Leon. *Why? Extermination Camp Lwow (Lemberg) 134 Janowska Street, Poland.* New York: Vantage Press, 1975.

Richman, Sophia. *A Wolf in the Attic: The legacy of a Hidden Child of the Holocaust.* New York: The Haworth Press, 1991.

Wells, Leon W. *The Janowska Road.* New York: Macmillen, 1963.

INDEX

INDEX

Part VI

APPENDIX

Fryderyka Mangel, nee Kessler,
Rzeszow, Poland, 1928

Mangel Family Picnic.
Rzeszow, Poland. August 18, 1928

Ryszard and Laura Kessler,
Lwow, 1930

Judge Pawel Kessler,
died in Winnica, 1940

Dr. Edmund Kessler,
Lwow, 1937

Fryderyka Kessler, nee Mangel,
Lwow, Poland 1937

Certificate to Practice Law, Edmund Kessler,
Lwow, Poland, 1937

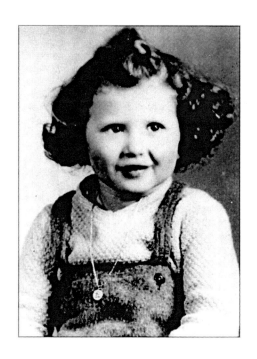

Renata Kessler`s Passport Photo,
Vienna, Austria, 1952

Edmund Kessler (second row, second on right)
with staff of Rothschild Hospital,
Vienna, 1950

Edmund Kessler at the World Jewish Congress,
approx. 1950

Katarzyna Kalwinska at postwar holiday celebration
with survivors of the bunker,
Poland, 1944 or 1945.
Katarzyna Kalwinska seated at center,
Edmund and Fryderyka Kessler on right

Kalwinski Family,
Gliwice, Poland, approx. 1960

Kalwinski Family house,
postwar, Lviv, Ukraine

AMERICAN JOINT DISTRIBUTION COMMITTEE

WÄHRINGERSTRASSE 2, VIENNA IX, AUSTRIA

American APO Address:

c/o Foreign Accrediting Office
Liaison Branch — Usooa — USCOA
APO 777, c/o P.M. New York

Telephone: A 19 5 45
Cables: Jointfund Vienna

Vienna, March 15, 1952.

TO WHOM IT MAY CONCERN.

Dr. Edmund KESSLER was associated with the International Committee for Jewish Refugees and Concentration Camp Internees from 1946 until March 1952. He served in the capacity of secretary and later as chairman.

This committee administered the refugee camps in Vienna including camp Rothschild through which were processed over 200,000 Jewish refugees. The committee worked with a high degree of efficiency and helpfulness overcoming great obstacles. Their cooperation with this organization was on the highest level throughout.

The degree of cooperation attained was largely attributable to Dr. Kessler who throughout his period of service demonstrated great administrative ability and a complete understanding of the problems. The committee and Dr. Kessler personally were held in high regard by the many organizations dealing with the problem of Jewish refugees. These included besides the American Joint Distribution Committee the U.S. High Commission, the Austrian Government and the IRO.

Dr. Kessler has resigned in order to emigrate to the United States. With him go our best wishes for every success in his new home.

Harold Trobe
Director
AJDC – Austria.

HT/HH

Letter from American Joint Distribution Committee,
by Director Harold Trobe

Breinigsville, PA USA
24 March 2010
234862BV00003B/1/P